WILLOW VALE FROME

Its Buildings Industries and People

By Derek Gill and John Buckley

Published by Frome Society for Local Study 2010
Printed by Butler, Tanner & Dennis, Frome
Pre-Press by Alan Yeates
© Derek J Gill & John Buckley
ISBN 978-0-9565869-0-2

Acknowledgements

I wish to thank John Buckley, John Cheetham, Carolyn Griffiths, John Hedges, Geoffrey Jackson, Jeremy Walwin and Basil Wild for their help and encouragement, and other residents of the Vale who have answered my many questions. I am particularly indebted to my wife Jean for her patience and help with my computer. Finally I would like to thank Alastair MacLeay and the Frome Society for Local Study for publishing this book.

Derek J Gill 2009

Foreword

When Derek Gill moved with his wife Jean and 3 sons to 15 Willow Vale nearly 35 years ago he was a teacher at Selwood School. Like him I am proud to be custodian of one of Willow Vale's fine houses, and share his interest in the history of this fascinating and attractive part of Frome.

Derek's work over many years to preserve Frome's architectural heritage and history is well known and highly regarded. So too are his many articles and publications. Recent health problems prevented him from finishing this book and he turned to me for help. I hope that my editing, interpretation and additions do justice to the wealth of material he assembled.

The first part of the book sets the scene with an overview of Willow Vale; how it came to be, how it was, and how it is now. It tells something of its history, river and mills, wildlife and industries. The second part gives an account of each of the buildings along the Vale, their uses, owners and occupiers over the past 200 years. In Part 3 the detailed index should prove useful, particularly to family historians.

John H W Buckley 2010

CONTENTS

CONTENTS (Continued)

PART 3   BIBLIOGRAPHY, ILLUSTRATIONS, APPENDICES & INDEX

SKETCH MAP OF BUILDINGS IN WILLOW VALE (2010)

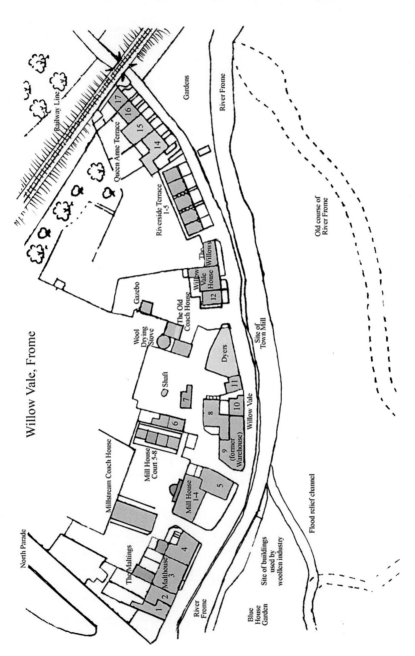

WILLOW VALE

Willow Vale is a cul-de-sac extending upstream from the Town Bridge in the west to the railway bridge and town meadow in the east. It brings a finger of countryside into the town centre and has been described as "Frome's green lung". An assortment of former workshops and warehouses sit cheek by jowl with fine houses, terraces and worker's cottages. These vernacular buildings are a microcosm of the Town's long history and association with the woollen and other industries. Nearly all appear on the 1813 map of Frome and some are of much earlier origin. Many were re-styled and updated in Georgian and Victorian times, a process that continues today. The only comparatively recent additions are Riverside Terrace and No. 12 built in the 1930s, and the Mill House Court development, completed in 2000. The Vale's crowning glory is the terrace of clothiers' houses built in the Queen Anne style.

The road was adopted for maintenance purposes by the County Council, but beyond "Dyers" is privately owned. Some of the houses here have gardens, garages or parking spaces on the riverbank, of which the owners are the riparian owners. Willow Vale was designated in 1982 as part of the Town's "Conservation Area" under the Town & Country Planning Acts. Its more recent designation as part of the "Sustrans" cycle route led to improvements to the footpath which runs from Wallbridge to the town centre. Since then there has been a marked increase in the number of pedestrians, cyclists and dog walkers using it for access to the town centre and for recreational purposes.

EARLY HISTORY

The 16th century brought great changes in the ownership of land in England following the closing of the monasteries. It provided an opportunity for a growing number of men who had made fortunes in the cloth industry, especially in this area, to buy and develop land acquired by the King. The Chantry lands of Our Lady in St John's Church were sold off to such self-made men who then developed them. Froome Selwood was a sheep farming area, and this was a time of growing prosperity in the cloth industry. Relatively flat areas of land were gradually filled. However, small pockets remained, much of it conveniently situated near the river Frome. So this is the story of how Willow Vale developed.

In the 13th century this area of Frome was known as Pylehewe, from the Old English "pilhlaw": a hill where wooden piles were obtained. On 19th century maps North Hill is shown as Pilly Hill. Until the 20th century Willow Vale was known as Pilly Vale. A few elderly townspeople still refer to it by this name.

RIVER, MILLS AND RAILWAY

The river Frome is not particularly impressive, yet tradition has it that there were once two hundred cloth mills on one six mile stretch. These must often have had to stop working because of the low level of water during prolonged dry spells, and there is evidence of prayers being said for rain. The river passes the remains of a number of these mills after entering the town at Wallbridge and taking its westerly course through water meadows, heath and woodland, past the buildings of Willow Vale to the Town Bridge.

Fed by a number of streams and springs it flows north-east, to meet the Avon between Avoncliffe and Freshford.

There have been three major changes to the river's course. A millstream was cut in the 16th century to serve the Town Mill. As can be seen from the 1813 map of Frome this was situated on an island opposite the building now known as "Dyers". It was used for  fulling (felting) cloth. The wooden pillars of the sluice which controlled its flow can still be seen near the railway bridge. A commemorative stone now housed in Frome Museum celebrates its refurbishment in 1847, but by 1880 it was derelict and the wheel and contents were sold at auction, together with other premises in Willow Vale.

It had been assumed that a complex of buildings located at the foot of the Blue House garden included a watermill. However an examination of 19th century maps shows no evidence for the existence of either a mill race or waterwheel. Together with the warehouse situated between Nos. 4 & 5 Willow Vale it was actually part of a complex of industrial buildings used for the manufacture of woollen cloth. A footbridge opposite No. 5 linked the two sets of buildings. The last remnants of the buildings were demolished in the late 1960s as part of the flood relief project.

As can be seen on maps up to the mid-20th century, the river's original course meandered through fields and gardens to the south of the millstream. It disappeared under the industrial expansion of Merchants Barton, Nott's Industries, and more recently the houses of River's Reach and car parks of Saxonvale. The millstream became the river's main channel, effectively forming the landscape of Willow Vale as we see it today.

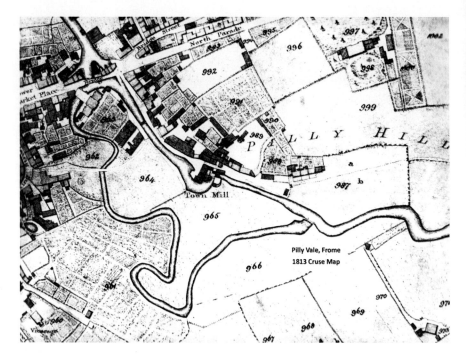

Pilly Vale, Frome
1813 Cruse Map

The planned route of the Radstock to Frome branch railway line is shown on the 1838 map of Frome. Two bridges were built in Willow Vale to carry the line over the footpath and river, resulting in a second diversion of the river's course. Opened by the Great Western Railway Company to freight traffic in 1854, the line was used mainly carrying coal from the North Somerset coalfield. It also carried cheese and other agricultural produce from Frome to markets in London. Narrowed from Brunel's broad gauge to the standard gauge in 1874 it carried passengers from 1875 until 1959. It no longer reaches Radstock, is now privately owned, and used almost exclusively to transport stone from the Mendip quarries onto the main rail network.

For the most part the river is a benign, gently flowing stream, but after heavy rain it can quickly become a raging torrent. It has also taken lives. The "Somerset Standard" of 13th May 1932 records how 5 schoolboys were playing in Willow Vale shortly before 4 o'clock, fascinated by the river which was in flood. They were standing on a stone archway, a remnant of the Town Mill, which connected the bank to a small island in the middle of the river near Willow Vale House. Without warning the masonry suddenly collapsed into the water carrying the boys with it. A police constable made a plucky but unsuccessful rescue attempt. One of the boys was rescued but the other four were swept away to their deaths under the Town Bridge. After the tragedy the last remains of the Mill were demolished.

The river was responsible for periodic flooding of the town centre. Because of the frequency with which this happened a number of houses have their principal living rooms on the first floor. The last serious flood in December 1960 was recorded in detail in the *"Somerset Standard"*. Traffic was diverted across the Bailey bridge and into Cork Street. The Blue Boar Inn had its ground floor flooded. Its landlord and his wife were confined to upstairs rooms. Accounts of the way in which individual properties and their occupants in Willow Vale were affected are described below.

Flood-prevention measures completed in the early 1970s deepened the

channel and controlled the flow, causing a third change in the river's course. The scheme has proved to be highly effective, but at the time of its construction was an environmental disaster. Riverbed dredging and the creation of a new channel round the Blue House garden to the "Blue Boar Inn" left barren ditches. The work destroyed most of the riverside vegetation including many splendid alder, copper beech, horse chestnut trees. With the passage of time these have regenerated. A dedicated group of local volunteers, "Friends of the River Frome", now undertake work to enhance the appearance of the riverbank.

CREATURES GREAT AND SMALL

Few towns can have such a plethora of wildlife so close to their centres. There are grey squirrels, water-voles, and occasional sightings of what could have been otters or mink. It is worth rising early on a spring morning to hear the magnificent dawn chorus. Both resident and migrant birds inhabit the Vale. Apart from the more common species such as its resident colony of ducks (mainly mallard); ring doves, heron, kingfishers, owls, willow warblers and woodpeckers are all observed quite frequently. Following snowfall tracks have been seen leading to an extensive badgers' sett in the Town Meadow. Perhaps the most exotic creatures to visit the Vale were elephants. When the circus was in town in the 1930s they came down the slipway, which then existed alongside the Town Bridge, to drink and bathe.

INDUSTRY AND BUSINESS

During the 18th and 19th centuries the Vale would have been a hive of activity. Frome was famous for the dyeing, weaving and finishing of woollen cloth. At the end of the 18th century there were 47 clothiers in Frome. Most were in a small way of business but the Sheppard family came to dominate the industry. During the 18th and early 19th centuries the firm's assets and activities were centred on Willow Vale. Cloth was processed in buildings they owned at the foot of the Blue House garden. Access was via a small footbridge opposite No. 5. Fulling was done upstream at the Town Mill. They also rented the workshop and warehouse between Nos. 4 and 5, the Willow Vale dyehouse and other premises from the Olive family. Under the stewardship of George Sheppard, the business expanded with the acquisition of mills and factories in other parts of the town. By the 1850s they had virtually ceased operations in Willow Vale, and moved their headquarters to Sheppard's Mill in Spring Gardens.

A visitor in 1808 described *"all the people of Frome being dyed purple with the manufacture of blue cloth"*. For 150 years the extensive dyehouse, which at its peak employed over 50 men, undoubtedly had a great impact on life in Willow Vale. It was built by Henry Allen, and operated by that family until 1796 when it was acquired by Major John Olive. There were similar premises in Justice Lane. For the next 80 years the Olive family owned virtually all the property along the Vale, from No. 4 to beyond Willow Vale House. Major John's nephew, John Olive V, managed these assets until his death in 1865. Other activities in the Vale included building, malting, the manufacture of feather pillows, sacks and organs, stables and a fleet of horse-drawn vehicles which provided transport for the Town's people and industry.

A couple of hundred years ago a stroll down Willow Vale would not have been the pleasant experience it is today. Your senses would have been assailed by the noise of the fulling mill's hammers, smells of fermenting vats and stale urine emanating from the dyehouse and stables' manure heaps. The river itself would have been an open sewer until a few years after the River Pollution Prevention Act of 1876. No doubt you would have been glad to leave quickly once your business transactions were finished.

With the decline of the cloth industry in the 19th and 20th centuries, many of the Vale's industrial buildings became redundant and derelict. These provided low rent accommodation for new businesses. In 1922 John White established Somerset Smithy in the old stables in Grant's Yard. In the remaining dyehouse workshop Willow Motors began trading, followed 35 years ago by Barnes' motor vehicle body repair shop. Frome Reclamation began trading in Grant's Yard. From small beginnings these businesses have flourished and moved to other, more spacious premises elsewhere around the town.

Now the Vale is a quiet, attractive, mainly residential backwater. Longstanding residents have befriended newcomers, and the place has a welcoming community spirit. Its recent inhabitants have included a wide range of professional people and artisans. Among these are artists, craftspeople and writers, an expert on early clocks, carpenters, clergy, doctors, dentists, nurses, teachers, and specialists in new technology. Its dwellings are particularly popular amongst people seeking tranquil retirement homes within easy reach of the town's facilities. During the past two decades the increase in property values has led to a flurry of renovation and restoration projects. The fabric of Willow Vale has never been in better shape.

HOUSE NUMBERING PROBLEM

Despite having access to the records listed in the bibliography, there are problems which make it difficult to identify with certainty the people who lived in specific dwellings. This particularly affects the smaller tenements located at the rear of No. 4 and Nos. 6 to 11 Willow Vale. The absence of a proper house numbering system prior to the introduction of the penny post in 1840 proved to be a handicap in dealing with earlier censuses. Frome's directories used their own inconsistent numbering systems which omitted many smaller dwellings. For example No. 15 Willow Vale appeared as number 8 in 1903, 11 between 1905 and 1911, and 12 in 1912. Its present house number first appears in 1918.

Before the building of North Parade, the first few houses along the Vale were known as "Bridge Row". Its cottages were substantially remodelled early in the 19th century. There are instances where the upper parts of one house extend over an adjacent property, leading to so called "flying freeholds". Smaller properties were amalgamated into larger ones and vice versa, and multiple-occupancy was not uncommon. This creates additional problems in interpreting the data.

PART 2   BUILDINGS, INDUSTRY AND PEOPLE

ENTRANCE TO WILLOW VALE

The Blue House and Town Bridge in 1996

At the entrance to Willow Vale stand two of Frome's most imposing and celebrated structures. "The Blue House", topped by its bell tower and clock was opened in 1724 to provide an almshouse: *"for poor women of the Parish"* and the *"Bluecoats Boys' School"*. Following a public appeal in 1965 the building was saved from demolition. Following major renovations the refurbished building was officially opened by Prince Charles on 6th June 1995. After nearly 300 years it still provides a comfortable home for some of Frome's elderly residents.

The Town Bridge has been remodelled several times. The one we see today was built in 1821 as part of Frome's new main through road, to a design by the County Surveyor, G. A. Underwood. It is remarkable in being one of only 3 bridges in England to have buildings on the spans, the others being in Bath and Lincoln.

On the far side of The Bridge are Frome Museum (formerly the Literary & Scientific Institute), the Black Swan Arts Centre, and the Tourist Information Centre, housed in a converted wool drying stove. The Market Place and shops are within a few minutes' walk. To the rear of the Vale is the thickly wooded slope of North Hill, or Pilly Hill as it was formerly known, with its fine mansion, railway line, and Telephone Exchange which provides a dominant but unsympathetic backdrop to the Vale.

The Vale's riverside guardrails and gas lamp standards were made at the Cockey Ironworks in Frome. Designed by the local art metal firm of Singers, the lamp heads are ornamented in art nouveau style. Now powered by electricity they have been given Grade II listing.

THE 1785 CENSUS OF HOUSEHOLDS

The earliest record of the owners and tenants of property along the Vale is *"The 1785 Census of Households"*. 13 households were listed in Bridge Row and 14 in Pilly Vale giving a total of 27. When the Riverside Terrace, built in the 1930s, and more recent conversions to residential use of stables, warehouses and workshops are taken into account, the total number of dwellings in Willow Vale is now around 40.

In 1785 the Vale's total population was 112 (52 males and 60 females). 12 of the dwellings were owned by M Griffith (a dyer), 7 by John Adlam (baker), 2 by Henry Allen (dyer), 2 by Josiah Ames (clothier), 2 by a Mrs Beard, and 1 each by Mary Gifford and Thomas Griffith (dyer). With 12 heads of household described as dyers or dyehousemen and 2 as shearmen, their occupations reflect the nature of industry in the Vale at that time. Most would have been employed in the dyehouses here or across in Justice Lane. "Shearmen" is a term applied to workers who used large shears to provide a final finish to woollen cloth. There is an interesting exhibit in Trowbridge Museum illustrating this highly skilled craft.

The corner house adjacent to the Town Bridge was demolished around 1797 when North Parade was constructed. In 1785 John Adlam, a baker, was living there with 3 other males and 6 females. It was subsequently rebuilt as No. 1 North Parade, or Pig Street as the lower part was previously known. In 1808 his executors were arranging the sale of his other houses in the Vale.

1 WILLOW VALE

Architecture

Evidence points to a 17th century date making it one of the oldest houses in the Vale. This includes the reeded mouldings on the stair risers of the winder stairs and gables. To the right of the ground floor window is evidence of a small blocked window which perhaps gave light to the bottom of the stairs. The main living room is now at the front of the house on the 1st floor and has a large Bath stone fireplace with a recess to one side, thought to be a wig cupboard. The property was given Grade II listing in 1974. It was described as: *"Late c17 altered. 2½ storey, gabled front in coursed rubble. Pantile roof. One 3-light window with chamfered mullions and drip*

in gable. Mid c19 windows below, 3 on 1st floor, cross-glazed sashes, one on ground floor, 16 pane sashes. 6 panel door to left with brackets to moulded flat hood. Interior: winder staircase, some risers are moulded."

In November 1902 the house was described in the auction catalogue as a: *"Freehold house with walled-in lawn and kitchen garden, containing – Ground floor: entrance hall, drawing room (about 12 x 15 feet), dining room (about 18 x 12 feet), kitchen fitted with range, larder, wash house, coal and wood house, and large workshop. First floor: – front bedroom (about 17 x 16 feet), 2 other bedrooms, 1 having a large closet. Second floor: – 2 attics. Frontage: – 23 feet to Pilly Vale".*

Owners and Occupiers

The 1727 rates list: *"Henry Allen for part of Pilly Hill or occupier William Denmead 9d".* The 1770 rates record: *"William Green attorney late Allen 'on the bridge' 6¼d"*. This confirms its position as the second property of the terrace, that William Palmer was in possession by 1785, and that William Green occupied the corner house. In 1785 the property was described as *"That messuage, with offices and garden adjoining, now in the tenure of Charles Palmer, heretofore in occupation of Henry Allen, after Henry Greene, John Gibbons, John Saunders or John Phillips as tenants, situate near the town bridge, late in the occupation of William Palmer deceased, together with an equal share of the wall between the dwellinghouse late in the tenure of John Adlam deceased and the said messuage of Charles Palmer."* This confirms the house to be the first in Willow Vale, the corner one being in North Parade.

In 1785 William Palmer was living here with 2 other males and 2 females. A plumber, painter and glazier, he purchased 1 Willow Vale from John Adlam's executors in 1808. His second son, Nicholas Palmer, was a cardboard maker (boards for carding wool), who owned Nos. 29 and 30 Naish's Street. Charles Palmer (1758-1838) succeeded his father in 1798 and like him was a painter. Listed in the 1821 Church rates as owner/occupier he is paying 8¼d rates. He had married Ann Gough in 1790 and had two children. He died on 23rd March 1838 aged 79. Charles' son Edward Palmer (1791-1877) inherited the house and business and is listed in the 1841 and 1851 censuses. He played the flute at Rodden Church, was churchwarden in 1842 and "Overseer of the Poor" for Frome Tithing. Edward married twice, first in 1819 to Elizabeth Wilton Hooper (1796-1853) by whom he had two children (Ann and Martin) who both died in their twenties. Ann married George Edwin Monk, a distinguished musician, who was organist at York Minster for 28 years, and a composer of settings for psalms. Edward's second marriage was to Emma Brake from Bath in 1855 when he was 63. Emma continued to live in the house after her husband's death and is recorded as a widow living with a servant in censuses and directories from 1881 to 1894. The house was auctioned following her death on 16th June 1897. The Palmer family had owned the house for over 100 years and had lived there for even longer.

Arthur John Jackson was an ironmonger in Frome Market Place. In 1897 he and his brother leased the ground floor of what is now the Stroud & Swindon Building Society for 2 years at £75 per annum. Jackson & Sons are listed in the 1907 local directory as ironmongers, trading at 1 Market Place. An advertisement on the front cover lists *"tools and cutlery, furnishings; the ironmongery; also bookseller and stationer"*. He purchased the freehold of 1 Willow Vale on 6th September 1897 for £257.13s from George Ashby, the surviving executor of Edward Palmer. At an auction on the previous 7th July Edwin John Jelly made the highest bid, but Ashby later agreed the sale to Arthur Jackson for the same price.

Jackson moved in and is listed there in the 1898 directory and until 1901. He spent £143 on improvements and must have been disappointed when it fetched only £205 at an auction in 1902. The purchaser was Alfred George Hayman of Hapsford House. William Hiscocks was the occupier as tenant to Hayman and is listed here in the 1905 and 1907 directories (there is no entry for 1903-1905) but by 1908 he had moved to 23 Keyford.

A. BOWSHER
13 Market Place
GENERAL IROMONGERY
Of Every Description.

Alfred Bowsher is in residence in 1908 and must have purchased the freehold. He was an ironmonger with a shop at 13 Market Place. He placed the above advertisement in the 1907 directory. By July 1912 Alfred had died and his widow conveyed the freehold to Augustus Dodge who was a boot and shoe maker of 1 Stony Street. His daughter had probably married Alfred Bowsher's son Alfred. Augustus may have been acting as executor, but in any case he too died shortly after, on 29th October 1912.

Mrs Smith, a dressmaker and milliner is listed at 1 Willow Vale between 1914 and 1917. Previously she had lived at 1 High Street, and by 1918 was at 43 Portway. Frederick Conduit is listed in the 1926 local directory, having previously lived at 7 Cheap Street. Herbert Thomas Paget is listed in directories between 1926 and 1960, having been the licensee of the White Hart Inn, a property owned by his brother-in-law, Charles William Sutton. Herbert was a noted billiard and snooker champion. They were badly affected by the flooding of December 1960. The *"Somerset Standard"* reported: *"Mr & Mrs H. T. Paget live alone, and nearly 3 feet of water entered the house, both back and front. Their son-in-law, Mr Malcolm Kirby came down on Sunday morning and was stranded with them in the upper rooms as the water rose rapidly. They had no breakfast, dinner or tea, and were unable to eat anything until late evening. The electric light failed and it was not possible to light the gas in the oven. They put the damage at £100 and express their gratitude to the council for providing fuel for the drying out process."*

The property was inherited in 1966 by Anne, daughter of Mrs Paget, who sold it to Mr & Mrs Lewis for £1,300 in October 1971. In September 1975 it was purchased by Sue Roman for £8,000. Miss Roman was an architect, and began modernising and restoring the property, especially the kitchen area. She married another architect, Tim Clarke, in 1977. In December 1980 she sold it and moved away. Over the next 8 years the house was to have 6 owners: the Parkers, Marsdens, Robinsons, Capt. Richard Franklin RN, and the Hutchins. In November 1988 the house was bought by John Curtis and his wife. They moved to Taunton and sold the house to Pip and Janis Leedam. Pip died, and in 2006 Mrs Leedam sold the house to its latest owners, Michael Bull and Ruth Massey.

2 WILLOW VALE

Architecture

Awarded Grade II listing in 1974, the house was described as: *"Late 18c front. Coursed and dressed rubble, cornice and parapet. 2 storeys and attic. 2 windows, 19c sashes in reveals. Right and left-hand door openings with stone slab hoods on brackets. Pantile roof with a late 19c gabled dormer. Gabled extension to rear with ovolo mullion (circa 1700) 2-light gable window."* The second door to the right gives access to a passageway to the rear of the

property. The hoods on both doorways are similar to those over the front doorways of Nos. 1 and 3, and the front elevations of both 2 and 3 Willow Vale are very similar in style. This resulted from a Regency re-modelling of the two properties around 1810 whilst under the ownership of maltster Thomas Balne.

Owners and Occupiers

In 1785 the house was owned by John Adlam the baker, who at the time of the 1808 rates is *"deceased"*. The tenants then were probably James Clark, a clockmaker and John Blatchley, a labourer. Following Adlam's death Thomas Balne acquired and re-built the property but by 1821 George Stile had become the owner/occupier, and was required to pay the Church 8¼d in rates. At the time of the 1841 census Sarah Herridge 50, a carrier, William Herridge 25, a woolstapler, Henry Backhouse 20, also a carrier, John Bebby 20, a draper's assistant, and B Harris an 18 year old servant, are living here. It may also be that John Palmer, a 70 year old weaver and his wife Elizabeth aged 80 are also living here or at No. 3. The Church rates for 1846/1850 show John Adams as the new owner and William Fairbanks, a solicitor from Wellow in Nottinghamshire, as tenant. Fairbanks is also listed in the 1851 census aged 68, with his wife Frances 74 and daughter Eliza 36, an unmarried schoolteacher.

According to the 1861 census Richard Edward Collins 34, a county court bailiff, previously living in Vallis Way, is tenant here with his wife Lydia, 6 children and a servant. He and his family appear again in the 1871 census by which time two of his children are working, one as a milliner and another as a brewery clerk. The house was uninhabited at the time of the 1881 census and no occupants are listed in the 1879, 1882 and 1890 directories or the 1889 poor rate. In 1891 William Hugnell 30, a domestic gardener from Frampton Cotterell in Gloucestershire, is living here with his wife Elizabeth 32 and two daughters. There is no listing in Frome directories for 1894, 1899, 1903 or 1912.

At some stage, possibly when he acquired the Maltings next door in the late 1860s Alfred Richard Baily became the owner of No. 2. It was auctioned as part of his estate in 1910 and purchased for £75 by E Baily & Sons when it was let to Mrs Sara Ann Sheppard at an annual rent of £10.10s.0d. She also appears in the 1910 voters list. George Bennett is in continuous occupation from 1915 to 1937, followed by W H Dixon. Miss F Wheeler and Miss L G Watts, dressmakers, are in residence from 1948 to 1961, sharing with Walter Wheeler and E M Peckham from 1955 to 1959.

At the time of the 1960 floods the "Somerset Standard" reported: *"Misses Watts and Wheeler living at No. 2 had the water in the house at 9 am on Sunday morning, and it rose to a height of three feet in the lower rooms. The floor coverings were damaged and furniture was also affected. They were able to make a cup of tea, but for most of the time had to remain upstairs. It was three years ago that a similar incident occurred. Of the decorations on the other side of the river, Miss Watts said that half a crib was swept away, together with several of the gnomes and at some time the water was up to the witch's chin as she peered round the trunk of a small tree"*.

E H Nutley followed in 1970, and S P Norwell (trading under the "Sign of Aquarius") in 1974. The 1979 voter list includes Simon Stubbs and Carolyn Woodthorpe. Adrian Leonard moved here from Milton Keynes with his young sons Giles and Tim and held the tenancy for a number of years prior to purchasing the property from his landlord's estate in 2007.

3 WILLOW VALE (The Maltings)

Architecture & Industry

The Malthouse and Maltings at the rear were given Grade II listing in 1974 when the property was described as: *"Late 18th/early 19th century. Possibly an 1821 remodelling of a house shown on 1813 map. Coursed dressed rubble, cornice, parapet, mansard roof, 2 hipped dormers, 2 storeys, 4 windows, c19 sashes in chamfered reveals, and chamfered door openings with ledged doors on each floor. Long, low 2½ storey maltings to rear with mansard roof, gable for hoist in centre, timber lintels"*.

There is evidence for a 16th or early 17th century cottage existing on the site. In the passage between the two properties the remains of its steeply pitched gable end can be seen on the wall of No. 2. There was also a gap between Nos. 3 and 4 as a blocked up window faces into the kitchen of No. 2 The Malthouse.

Following Thomas Balne's acquisition of the property in 1808 the cottage was demolished and a Regency style town house erected in its place. The garden was in the form of a long, narrow triangle with its point extending beyond the Masonic Hall. He built a 2-storey stone floor maltings on this land, measuring 18 x 96 feet, and at right angles to this a grain store. A walkway in the passage between Nos. 2 and 3 at 1st floor level enabled sacks of malt and grain to be hoisted on to and off horse-drawn wagons waiting below.

The Maltings would have supplied Frome's numerous inns and alehouses, which at that time would have been brewing their own beer. These small backyard concerns gradually amalgamated into larger breweries like Frome United and the Lamb Brewery. The quantities of malt required increased, and when Baily's new maltings were built near the railway station, smaller maltings like those in Willow Vale became uneconomic.

Like so much ornamental ironwork, the railings set into the stone wall surrounding the narrow front garden were removed in the 1940s to help the War effort. After the war the house was converted into two horizontal flats. In 1977 the Rathmells sold most of the rear garden to the Trustees of Frome Masonic Hall, and in 1982 permission was granted to demolish part of the Maltings to provide space for the Masonic car park. In the late 1980s John Potter of Limpley Stoke bought the property and commissioned Mr

Andrews, a director of The Real Stone Company of Bath, to draw up plans for a major renovation of the site. The conversion was done sympathetically and to a high standard, creating two 3-storey town houses (Nos. 1 & 2 The Malthouse), and a further dwelling at the rear in the remaining part of the Maltings.

The Maltings The studded oak door (not original) in the passage between Nos. 2 and 3 Willow Vale gives access. On the ground floor there was a courtyard atrium and living room/kitchen. The latter was relocated in the atrium in 2008. There is a bedroom and bathroom on the first floor, and a further bedroom with en-suite shower and wash basin on the second floor.

No. 1 The Malthouse This was formed from the left half of the Malthouse, and is entered by a door in the passage to the right of the entrance to The Maltings. Original Regency style features have been retained in the living room. These include arched recesses on either side of the fireplace and a reeded architrave and shutter boxes around the window. In addition to the living room

there is a hall, cloakroom/toilet and kitchen/diner on the ground floor, two bedrooms, bathroom and shower room on the first floor, and two further small bedrooms and a large studio in what was formerly the kiln, on the second floor. The louvered ventilator, which once controlled the heat in the kiln, has been converted into a tent-shaped glazed lantern above the studio.

No 2 The Malthouse The right-hand half of the Malthouse retains the original front door with its canopy similar to those on the first two houses. On the ground floor there is a living room with a Victorian fireplace, a kitchen/ diner and shower/toilet. There are 2 bedrooms and shower/toilet on the first floor, two further bedrooms and a bathroom on the second floor. Both Nos. 1 and 2 The Malthouse have small terraced gardens at the rear.

Owners and Occupiers

John Adlam owned the old cottage at 3 Willow Vale at the time of the 1785 census, when it was probably rented by a breeches maker, John Stevens, with four males and a female living there. When Thomas Balne acquired the property from Adlam's estate in 1808, he re-modelled the house, built the maltings, and employed a series of maltsters to manage the business. Thomas Sparks was the first and is listed in the 1810 rates. In 1821 Mrs Sparks is running the business and paying 9½d in Church rates for the house, and 7½d for the maltings. The 1827 Church Rates list Henry Bebby as tenant of the house and Thomas Vaters as the maltster, followed in the 1841 census James Vaters 40, living here with his brother Henry 43 and sister Mary Vaters 45, plus a servant. Thomas Balne's wife Mary is listed as owner in the 1846/1850 Church rates with Thomas Vaters again listed as maltster/tenant. At the time of the 1851 census James Vaters is back as maltster with his brother and sister, now aged 56, 60 and 62 respectively, and a servant (Louisa Baily) and 2 men.

From the 1868 Electors' Roll we learn that the new owner of the maltings is Edmund Baily, a local farmer, grain merchant, maltster and innkeeper. He installed his son Alfred Richard Baily here as maltster, employing 4 men. Alfred 26, his wife Mary Susanna, daughter Mary and a servant are listed here in the 1871 Census, and again in the 1879 directory. When Edmund became part owner of Baily's maltings near the railway station he decided to sell the maltings in Willow Vale. The auction took place on 6th October 1880 but the property failed to reach its reserve price of £750.

Following Edmund's death in 1881 his son Alfred moved to Willow Vale House. The uninhabited property was re-advertised with a reserve of only £450. He offered to rent the maltings from the new owner for £15 per annum but it still did not sell. The maltings fell into disuse but the Malthouse had a series of tenants including Mrs Louisa Knight, a widow born in Buenos Aires, the Rev Frank W Vining, a curate at St John's Church, and Bernard J Mitchell from 1903 to 1927. Further information on the Baily family can be found under Willow Vale House and on Bernard Mitchell under 15 Willow Vale.

A Mrs Blades is living here in 1929, S A Smith in 1930, H F G Thomas in 1936, and R V Allen in 1937. No directories were published during the War when the property was divided into two horizontal flats. Between 1948 and 1955 W H Dixon, C Mountier, and B Hiscox were here. Mountier appears again in 1961. In 1962 the property was sold by Samuel Thompson & Sons to David and Kathleen Rathmell. David was a solicitor, and partner in the firm of Ames, Kent & Rathmell. In 1970 Mrs D M Cooke lived in 3a and A W Bray in 3b, followed by Mrs Richards and Mrs Shipley. Bray, a brother of Ellen Bray, was proud of his flat and its architecture. When speculative "antique dealers" enquired about purchasing the original oak staircase, he turned them away.

In 1983 ownership passed to the Rathmell's son Timothy who owned a gift shop in the Town. Five years later he sold it for £77,000 to John Potter, a property developer from Limpley Stoke, who undertook its conversion into the three dwellings described above.

A local general practitioner, Dr Philip DeGlanville became the first owner/occupier of The Maltings. In 2002 he sold it to his godson, Christopher Huxley-Reynard as a home for his mother Barbara Huxley, an artist, who has since moved round the corner to 6 Mill House Court. Mark Willis became the owner in 2006.

In June 1990 Ben and Elizabeth Gale became the first owners of the newly refurbished No. 1 The Malthouse, and lived here with their 5 children for 2 years. Ben was a stonemason who had been working on the building. They were followed in May 1992 by two young doctors, Justin Phillips and Sarah Burford. John and Jennifer Buckley acquired the property in September 1994. John was a retired health service planning officer, and Jenny had been an art teacher.

The Rev John & Jill Huggins purchased No. 2 The Malthouse in April 1994 from its first owners, Neil Hewlett and Susan Loveridge. The Rev Huggins died in May 1999 and is buried at East Woodlands.

4 WILLOW VALE (Grant's House)

Willow Vale from Town Bridge c1880 - watercolour by unknown amateur.

Architecture

A 16th or 17th century cottage existed on the site prior to the 19th century with small tenements attached to the rear. A blocked-up window with ovolo mouldings faces into the kitchen of No. 3; evidence that a gap once existed between Nos. 3 and 4. The sketch above shows scaffolding erected on the front of 4 Willow Vale during a late Victorian re-modelling of the house, probably to a design by William George Brown (architect). This completed the terrace of Nos. 1 to 4 much as we see it today.

In 1880 the house was advertised as being *"Newly built"* and when John Olive's executors auctioned the property on in 1910 it was described as having: *"a flower garden in front and kitchen garden of about 20 perches at the rear, with extensive stabling, coach houses, four storey warehouse and stable yard with substantial 8-roomed dwelling house, the whole having a 147 ft frontage to the road and a depth of 156 ft. The residence contains: Basement: a large cellar. Ground floor: entrance hall, drawing room 16 x 14 ft, dining room 16 x 14 ft, kitchen 15 x 13 ft, china pantry, back kitchen and larder. First floor: 4 bedrooms, dressing room, W.C. Second floor: 3 bedrooms and large cupboard."* It did not sell.

Given Grade II listing in 1974 the building was described as: *"Circa 1880 in Jacobean Gothic style. Coursed rubble. 2 storeys and 2 attics in gables with copings and finials, 3 windows, 2-light stone mullioned casements, transoms to ground floor and 1st floor windows. Central door, ornate gabled stone porch, trefoil outer openings, pinnacles. Elliptical arched door opening with keystone. Panelled, half-glazed door".*

Owners, Occupiers and Industry

John Adlam was owner at the time of 1785 census, with shearman James Palmer as tenant in the main house, living with 2 other males and 3 females. Occupants of the cottages at the rear are listed below. Major John Olive acquired the property in 1796. According to the 1821 Church rates Joseph Harrold was tenant paying 7½d. It was inherited by Major John's nephew, John Olive V, who died in 1865, and appears to have remained part of his estate for some considerable time as it was auctioned in 1880 and again in 1910.

The Brown Family The 1827 rates show T Brown in residence. By the time of the 1841 census William Brown (1794-1861), a carpenter is tenant, living here with his wife Mary and their 10 children. He founded what became a prominent firm of Frome builders and is listed in the 1851 census as such. His third son Frederick Parfitt Brown (1825-1891) had taken over the tenancy by 1861. At that time the firm of F & W G Brown was employing 36 men and 4 boys. Frederick remained as tenant for the next 30 years until his death in 1891.

The Wall Family In his youth Thomas Wall was brought to Frome from Shepton Mallet by the proprietor of the George Hotel, and ran the Bull Hotel stables for several years (more recently the General Post Office). Posting master at 3 Bridge Street he moved to 4 Pilly Vale in 1892, as an advertisement in the local directory records.

LIVERY STABLES
4 Pilly Vale and George Hotel Yard, Frome
THOMAS WALL
Begs to announce his removal from Bridge Street to the above address
Open and Closed Carriages, Lock-up Coach House and Loose Boxes
Good Supply of Brakes for Pleasure Parties.
Funerals attended with closed or open car (Two or Four Horses).
Shillibeer, Mourning Coaches, Landaus and Broughams.

Thomas had 5 children by his first wife Sarah Jane and 3 by his second, Frances Amelia (Fanny). His obituary in the *"Somerset Standard"* records that: *"He established the Woolpack Stables in Trowbridge about 6 years before his death. He drove a team of 4 horses in the procession on the day before his death to celebrate the relief of Mafeking, which shows how suddenly the end came. On Monday 20th May 1900, the day after, he ate a moderate breakfast, went into the garden to cut some asparagus, and shortly after was taken ill with some internal pain, and died 20 minutes later. He had been in business for 23 years and had the largest stock of horses of any job master in the district, was upright in all his dealings, and knew a good animal when he saw it".*

After his death his widow Fanny continued to lease the property at an annual rent of £55 and ran the business until the start of the Great War in 1914. She had left by 1916 and died in 1945 at the age of 79. Between 1918 and 1920 George Tubbs was living here.

The Grant Family Thomas Grant (c1840-1915) was born at Corsley and his brother Charles at Upton Scudamore c1845. They came to Frome in 1871, first to the Market Place, then in 1875 to 23 King Street, and later to 6 North Parade. He probably acquired 4 Willow Vale at the 1910 auction of A R Baily's estate. Between 1889 and 1894 Charles John Grant, a sign painter, lived with his wife and large family at No. 5, and is also listed at No 14 in the directories from 1907 to 1920. They were known as the Grant Brothers, plumbers, painters, glaziers and paperhangers.

Of a musical family, Thomas had been organist at Chapmanslade's new parish church from 1867 to 1874, and shortly after moving to Frome in 1875, at the Wesley Church where he continued until his death in 1915. His wife Maria (1836-1931) bore him 5 sons and 5 daughters. Thomas senior's 3rd son, Thomas Grant jnr. (1877-1942), continued to run his father's business and is listed here in the 1927 and 1929 directories. As a boy he was a member of Christ Church choir and became a server at St John's, later joining its choir, which he regularly attended for 40 years. He was Treasurer of Frome Mechanics Institute and was described in his obituary as *"a man of sterling character; very strong-minded and difficult to move from his own course of action".*

An advertisement which appeared in the 1927 local directory shows that Thomas senior's eldest son, William J Grant (1866-1931), had a business

---

W. J. GRANT
Organ Builder, Tuner and Repairer
Estimates for New Organs, Tuning and Repair free on application
Fan Blowers Installed - 36 years experience
Workshops - Market Yard, Justice Lane
All communications to be addressed to:
4 WILLOW VALE, FROME

---

building and maintaining organs, with workshops located in Justice Lane. He gives 4 Willow Vale as his home address, so must have been living here with his younger brother Thomas. George Frederick Grant (born 1876), Thomas senior's second eldest son lived here from 1948 to 1957. He appears to have taken over his elder brother William's business as his name "G F Grant" appears in a photo of a Pianoforte & Organ showroom, which is thought to have been housed in the Feather Factory.

Miss Harriet Grant (born c1878), Thomas senior's daughter, was the last of the family to live here. At the time of the 1960 flood she would have been in her early 80s. The local paper mentioned that it was: *"the home of Miss Harriet Grant, with whom Mr & Mrs E J Turner also reside there. There was 8 inches of water all over the lower rooms, despite the fact that the front door is approached by 5 steps. There was mud left on all the floor coverings and furniture"*.

Grant's House Dental Surgery   Shortly after the Grants vacated the house, Anthony Brown moved his dental practice here from Stony Street. The practice flourished and this use of the building continues today. For a time the cottage at the rear was used as a dental technician's workshop, but the upper floor is now an additional dentist's surgery.

Tenements at rear of No. 4

In the 1785 census of households this dwelling housed 4 males and 3 females with Anthony Palmer, a shearman, as tenant paying 1½d rates. An extension was added to create a further dwelling. The 1821 Church rates list George Harrold as paying 1½d for the tenancy of one cottage and William Carter 2d for the other. William Carter appears again in the 1827 rates. The censuses and Church rates from 1841 to 1851 record a labourer, William Thorne, as tenant, together with his wife Sarah, a wool picker, and 2 children.

Following the 1880 refurbishment the dwellings appear to have been incorporated into the main house. At some stage the extension was demolished to provide access to the Masonic car park.

MILL HOUSE COURT (GRANT'S YARD)

Industry and Architecture

This prominent 4-storey building was used as a workshop and warehouse by Messrs. Sheppards. The large windows gave good light for the cloth workers. Earlier parish records list Sheppards as both owners and occupiers and when ownership transferred to the Olive family Sheppards continued as tenants until the middle of the 19th century. This may have been the building which was set on fire by rioters at a time of depression in the woollen industry in the early 19th century. It was rated at 7¼d and used for storage in 1821.

During the late 19th and early 20th centuries the warehouse building had a variety of uses. The Grant family repaired, displayed and sold organs here. It was used briefly for stuffing feather pillows (hence it's more recent name of the "Feather Factory") and for the display and sale of Hunter's wood burning stoves. The building was awarded Grade II listing in 1983. It was last used commercially as the premises of Frome Reclamation. When this firm moved to Station Approach the building was in a ruinous state. The upper floors were in a dangerous condition, the loft inhabited by pigeons, and Grant's Yard was a wilderness.

For about 60 years from 1827 other parts of the site were used as a builder's yard by F & W G Brown and for the following 20 years as livery stables by the Wall family. At the auction of John Olive V's estate in 1880 the premises at the rear of the No. 4 Willow Vale were described as: *"Stabling comprises 7 stall stables with loft over and harness room, range of 5 good loose boxes, two stall stables with loose box, harness room with loft over, coach house 61 x 25 ft, with hay and corn loft over, and workmens' W.C. Four-storey warehouse with ground area 50 x 20 ft and recently re-roofed, and stable yard 68 x 66 ft"*. The warehouse was then being used as a store by the Cockey Ironworks.

When J W Singer & Sons sold the art side of its business it became the Morris Singer foundry, now located at Basingstoke. The book *"A Century of Statues"* by Duncan James (1984) traces its history. Former employee John White, apprenticed to Singers during the Great War, opened his own foundry in part of the stables in Grant's Yard in 1922. Initially trading as John White & Son Ltd he renamed the firm "Somerset Smithy". It soon gained a reputation for the excellence of its ornamental ironwork and relocated later to its present premises in Christchurch Street West.

1 – 4 The Mill

Acting for the previous owner, Steve Horler of Frome Reclamation, architect Bruce Yoell drew up an inspired and sympathetic design to convert the building into four maisonettes. Access was to be via a new external winder staircase in a semi-circular turret, joined to the main building by a structure of oak balconies. The site was subsequently acquired by property developer Damien Kelly and attracted Heritage Lottery funding. After protracted negotiations with the Local Authority, permission to go ahead with the scheme was granted in 2000 and the contract was managed by Wolstenholme & Partners. Recent owners include Gary & Susan Carpenter in No. 1, Moira Chapman in No.2, Eleanor Smith in No. 3, and Lucinda Carr and Julian Quail in No. 4

5 – 8 Mill House Court

Kelly also built an attractive terrace of four new stone cottages in Grant's Yard. Owners include Patricia Harrison at No. 5 ("Willow Corner"), Barbara Huxley at No. 6, Geoffrey Willmott & Grace Barr at No. 7 ("Goose Feather Cottage"), and Andrew & Penelope Saunders at No. 8. The work, which took over 2½ years to complete was finished to a very high standard. An historic building has been saved and the the whole development, now renamed "Mill House Court", is an asset to Willow Vale.

Millstream Coach House

Located between Mill House Court and the Masonic car park this substantial rubble stone building measuring 61 x 25 feet originally had open brick arches at ground floor level with a hay and corn loft above. It was built as a coach house and used as such by Thomas Wall's livery stables. During the Great War and up until the 1920s the Fire Brigade kept their horses, fire engine and equipment here. Later it was used for storage. In the 1990s it was developed as a detached house with indoor swimming pool by Arthur Stevens, who named it "Premier House" and lived there with his partner. Jane MacGillivray bought it from Stevens, and lived there with her daughters in the late 1990s/early 2000s. Part of it was converted into a self-contained annexe to provide accommodation for her mother, Beatrice MacGillivray. Currently owned and occupied by the Tipper family, it has now been given the more appropriate name of "Millstream Coach House".

5 WILLOW VALE

Architecture

This once fine Georgian house stands to the right of the warehouse. In the 1940s, with the insertion of a second front door to the left of the original, the house was divided vertically to create Nos. 5 and 5a. Awarded Grade II listing in 1974, the 1983 Scheduled List describes it as: *"18th with early 19th century features. Ashlar, coved eaves cornice, moulded on return to right and to rear. Hipped pantile roof with central chimney. Plinth and corner piers. 2 storeys. 5 windows, some blocked with sash rebates, glazing bar sashes. Round-headed panel above door. Flush-panelled front door. Later door to left hand side".* There are indications of a missing triangular pediment or canopy over the original front door.

Around the year 2000 property developer Damien Kelly purchased the property and completely renovated both houses. The garden was divided into 3 plots, allocating one portion to No. 5, and the other two to the two lower maisonettes in the Mill House.

Owners and Occupiers

In 1785 the house was owned by Mary Gifford and let to a gentleman, Robert Bickle. By the time of the 1821 Church rates Major John Olive had become the owner and remained so until his death in 1827. Inherited by his nephew, John Olive V, it was auctioned as part of his estate on 2nd June in 1880 as Lot 6 *"with right of way for horses, carts and carriages"* but it went unsold at £400, and again in 1889 when it was described as a *"house with walled garden".* It was offered again for sale at an auction of John Olive junior's estate in 1910.

William Carter was the tenant in 1821, paying 2d rates and in 1827 the tenant was I Fisher. According to the *"Somerset County Gazette"* Sophia Underwood ran a girls' day school here, and is listed in the 1841 census as a 55 year old instructress, living with one pupil and a servant. Between 1846 and 1851 Henry Brown, a 56 year old wool-stapler is resident, and in 1861 James William Pratten, an engineer with his wife, daughter, and former servant Jane Sealy. Ten years later the census shows John Backhouse, a blue-black and medleywool dyer from Leeds living here with his wife and 9 children. By 1881 Maria Bryant, an innkeeper's wife is resident with 2 children and a servant, and in the 1879 and 1882 directories, Thomas Bryant is shown as tenant. One of the Grant brothers, Charles, a sign painter is listed as tenant in the 1889 poor rate, 1890 and 1894 directories. In the 1891 census he is aged 45 and living here with his wife Emma, also 45, their 4 sons and 5 daughters aged between 3 and 17. He later moved to No. 14. In 1899 the tenant was Mrs A E Organ, between 1903 and 1907 Walter Cutter, a gardener, and in 1912 H C Laverton. The house appears to have been unoccupied between 1920 and 1927, but Arthur G Miners was here between 1929 and 1937.

5a Willow Vale (Bridge View)

Following the division of the house into two, M S Knight was resident from 1948, followed by W Norman, and Mr & Mrs H Barnett from 1955 to 1961. A report of the 1960 flood shows that *"Mr & Mrs Barnett had 3 feet of water in their lower rooms. It came in on Sunday morning and receded at 4 pm. Mr Barnett could do little to move furniture as he was recovering from pneumonia and pleurisy."*

More recently the owners were Alick & Margaret Acott. After Alick's death, Margaret spent considerable time and energy feeding and sustaining a large population of mallard ducks on the river. Consequently she came to be known locally as the "Duck Lady". She moved briefly to the Blue House before joining her son John in Cornwall.

5 Willow Vale

Mr & Mrs H M Freyer were resident from 1955 to 1976. The 1960 flood report said *"Next door at No. 5 Mr & Mrs Freyer moved everything that could be moved upstairs. Their thoughtful daughter Mrs Lovegrove of Buckland Dinham brought them in two cooked dinners, which helped to see them through the day. Floor coverings were damaged but they had moved their carpets to safety."*

John Acott (son of Alick at No. 5a) was the owner from 1974 to 1980 until he left for Australia, and was followed from 1980 to 2000 by Jean Pollock & Eric Norman. They moved to Rivers Reach, where Eric died shortly afterwards. Both halves of No. 5 were then purchased by Damien Kelly.

6 TO 11 WILLOW VALE

In the 18th century the land on which these cottages were built belonged to Samuel Allen the dyer. When Major John Olive bought the freehold in 1796 it was described as: *"A dwellinghouse, dyehouses, stoves, and yard etc".* The 1880 auction of John Olive V's property in Willow Vale lists Lot 4 as: *"A block of buildings, dyehouses, stables, large yards, drying ground and a well-constructed and newly built shaft, and also newly built stores and counting house in occupation of Messrs Sheppard & Watson, cloth manufacturers of Pilly Hill".* The circular drying stove adjacent to The Old Coach House is similar in design to the one in Justice Lane which has been restored and now houses Frome's Tourist Information Centre. The remains of the well shaft can still be seen in the garden of No. 6.

Workers were housed in small cottages and tenements near the dyehouse. A number of buildings shown on the 1813 and 1838 maps of Frome have disappeared from the later Ordnance Survey maps. This and the lack of a proper house numbering system make it difficult to identify who lived where. Whilst we can be certain that the occupiers listed below all lived in this area at the time, some licence has been taken in attributing them to particular dwellings.

Following the auction of John Olive V's estate in 1880 T B W Sheppard acquired the properties. In 1906, four years before his death, he sold them to Hugh Lush, who after his death, left his estate to his wife Kate and two sons Hugh and Uriah. This later became part of the Witcomb Trust Legacy. In April 1923 Frederick Walwin, a Frome accountant living at 10 Vicarage Street, purchased the warehouse, counting house, Nos. 6 to 11 Willow Vale, and the surrounding garden plot. This is when the deeds and traceability of the individual properties start. Frederick Walwin senior died on 26th December 1952. Nos. 6, 7 and 8 were sold, but Jeremy Walwin inherited Nos. 9 and 10.

6 WILLOW VALE (The Old Kiln)

Architecture

This detached property to the rear of No. 5 faces southeast, with a garage facing southwest towards the river. When offered for sale in 1988 it was described as having a: *Hall, Cloakroom, Sitting Room 14ft 9ins x 14ft. Kitchen/Dining Room 15 x 13ft. and Utility room 9 x 7ft on the ground floor. Upstairs are 2 Bedrooms 15 x 12ft and 12 x 9ft and a Bathroom. Underneath is a cellar with arched ceiling measuring 40 x 14ft. It also has 2 garages and an attractive garden.*

Owners and Occupiers

In 1785 the cottage was owned by M Griffith and occupied by Miss Elizabeth Ford. Under the Olive family's ownership the Church Rates for 1821 show H Harrold as tenant, and Kemp in 1827. The 1841 census shows Henry Dyer, a 50 year-old labourer living here with his wife Sarah 50, sons William, an apprentice tailor, and Benjamin. The 1846/7 Church Rates record Elizabeth Olive as owner with Joseph Gunning as tenant. In 1851 a 61-year old widow and pauper, Sarah Wilkins is living here with her daughter Jane 27, an unmarried general servant. In 1861 a gardener and coachman from Melksham, George Tucker 60, lived here with his wife and daughter, and in 1871 Edwin Tucker

36, a coachman from Bradford with his wife Ann and 3 children. By 1881 John Penelhurn 55, a railway labourer from Devon is living here with his wife and 5 children. The 1891 census lists Ezra Grist 57, a general labourer from Corsley living here with his wife Oprah, their daughters Lucy and Emily, both 23 and laundresses, and 11 year-old son Leonard Edwin. Oprah Grist is still the tenant in the 1910 voters list, and Miss Lucy Grist through to 1937.

On 4th September 1945 Frederick Walwin sold the freehold to Arthur Henry and Jessie Warwick . They had lived here since 1942 and Jessie continued to do so after Arthur's death in 1956 and until she sold the cottage to Miss Constance May Jeffries on 26th March 1964. Five years later Miss Jeffries sold it to Peter Alexander MacQueen, who was probably the person who named the cottage "The Old Kiln". There were to be eight more owners over the next 30 years: Janet Scowcroft (1971-6), Edgar & Nancy Palmer (1976-89), John Ray (1979), Wessex Retirement Homes (1979-90), Martin A Cole (1990-96), Christiana Bamberg (1996-2002). The present owners, John & Sheila Hedges, moved there in 2002.

7 WILLOW VALE

Owners and Occupiers

This interesting detached cottage faces south onto 8 Willow Vale. Its deeds apply to No. 6 too. According to the 1785 census it was owned by M Griffith and occupied by a widow, Jane Griffiths and 2 maiden ladies. Frederick Walwin acquired the property in 1923. Little is known about the building but from Church and Poor Rates, Censuses and Frome Directories it is possible to compile a reasonably accurate list of tenants. The Dyer family occupied the cottage for over 30 years from around 1841; an apt surname given their occupations and the fact that the cottage was in the midst of the dyehouse complex.

1821-1827	Benjamin George
1841	Charles Dyer 55, a wool trader, wife Martha, and 6 children.
1846	Charles Dyer & family
1851	Charles Dyer 65, now a cloth dyer, his wife Martha 58 and daughter Ann 28, both wool pickers.
1861	Charles Dyer 75, now a wool drier stove man, with his wife and unmarried daughter Ann, both wool pickers.
1871	John Dyer 37, Charles' youngest son, a wool scourer, his wife Martha 38, a wool weaver, their 2 sons and 2 daughters.
1881	Charles Hurden 71, carter, and his wife Elizabeth 43.
1889-91	Tim Bush 47, groom, his wife Maria and their 4 children and stepson, Alfred Glass.
1910	Fred Whitmarsh (who was at No. 10 by 1927)
1930	Mrs Alice Neale
1934	Mrs E Neale
1936	Uninhabited
1937-1957	Mrs Rose M Goddard
1970-1994	Ivor H Treasure
2008	Susan Cullip

THE BUILDINGS AT 8 WILLOW VALE

This property opposite No. 7 backs onto Nos. 9 (the former warehouse) and No. 10. After 1861 there appear to have been 2 tenements and stables here. In the early 1960's glazier Alvan Jack Lee acquired the property from the Walwins and used the stable as his workshop until he retired in 1997. The buildings became derelict, and were purchased by property developer Arthur Stevens, who created 3 small cottages with 8b in the yard opposite No. 7, and 8 and 8a tucked into the corner.

8 Willow Vale

The corner part of the block was once the residence of the manager of the dyeing business. James Macey is listed in the 1821 and 1827 Church Rates. George Mills 38, a dyer, his wife Fanny, their 5 children and a servant appear in the 1841 census, but had moved to No. 10 by 1851. In 1861 Edward

Clough, a 39 year old wool cloth dye manager from Blumley in Yorkshire is in residence, with his wife Anne and daughter Jane Elizabeth. In 1871 it was occupied by Edward Harvey and his wife Louisa, a charwoman. Edward was a 50 year old Frome man, working at the dyehouse. Between 1889 and 1891 James Harebottle, a general labourer, was in residence, together with his wife Fanny and 4 children. The eldest of these, Annie 15, was a folder at the Print Works. Later electoral registers give us the following names: James Watts (1910), Walter Laverton (1927), Herbert Rogers (1929), W H Carpenter (1936-61), who moved to Wales to train for the priesthood, and Alvan Jack Lee (1970-79).

Following the 1997 restoration No. 8 contains a kitchen/ diner, sitting room, 2 bedrooms and shower room. Anne Parfitt became its most recent owner in 2006.

8a Willow Vale

Originally part of No. 8 and tucked away in the corner to its right, 8a was separated from that property in 1997 and renovated to form a unique cottage, which is now owned and occupied by Alan Davis.

8b Willow Vale

Records indicate that between 1821 and 1861 there was a second dwelling on this site. The 1821 and 1827 rates show James Budd as tenant. In 1841 John Goodland, a 48 year old labourer, was living here with his wife Hester 50

8b Willow Vale

and children James, Sarah and Jacob. The couple were still there a decade later but without their children. By 1861 John had died, and his wife Hester, an 84 year old widow, was living there with James Chinnock 66, a former dyehouseman, and his wife Rachel.

No further residents are listed after 1861, and the 1880 sale plan indicates that this part of No. 8 was a stable. Its cobbled floor could be seen before it was concreted over. Much later it became the workshop and glass store of Alvan Jack Lee, the glazier who worked here from 1961 until he retired in 1997. The old cobbled floor was covered with shards of glass. When the conversion to form a dwelling was taking place, many pieces of glass were deposited in the garden behind No. 7, but the rest was buried under the concrete floor before internal walls were built. The house, named "Ivy Lodge" now contains 3 bedrooms, a sitting room, kitchen/dining room and a bathroom, and is occupied by Shane Grimsley and Elizabeth Kingett.

9 WILLOW VALE (The Warehouse)

Architecture & Industry

Owned by the Olive family, in 1821 it was a hat manufactory let to John Nicholls of Portway, paying 2¼d church rates. From 1827 to 1882 the warehouse was leased to Messrs Sheppard & Watson. Following the demise of the cloth industry, the building was used for a variety of purposes. According to the 1889 poor rate the executors of Edward Cockey were renting the warehouse. In 1911 part was used by White Brothers, cheese factors, and from 1912 to 1934 as a cheese store for Wiltshire United Dairies. The painted advertisement recalls its later use by John Barrow, a sack merchant. Pillows were also made here.

When Jeremy Walwin inherited the property from his father he was faced with the problem of what to do with it. He initiated a conversion project for the whole terrace. The building was divided into three separate dwellings, each built with steps leading up to the front door to prevent flooding. Walwin also renovated No. 10, and now has tenants in all four dwellings. The whole terrace is a fine example of the modernisation and re-use of old buildings, and complements its Willow Vale setting.

9 Willow Vale (Pillow Cottage)

This is the interestingly shaped corner of the building, curved to accommodate the passage of horses and carts. It still bears Barrow's sack and feather advertisement, and has views across the river and to the Town Bridge.

9a Willow Vale

The next section of the terrace overlooks the river, and has large windows facing to the rear.

9b Willow Vale

This double-fronted terraced cottage also overlooks the river, but backs onto 8A at the rear.

9 and 10 Willow Vale

10 WILLOW VALE

This house to the right of the former warehouse has a side entrance between it and No. 11 and forms the end of the original terrace. Owned by Major John Olive, the Church rates for 1821 and 1827 indicate that his nephew, John Olive V was in residence. In 1841 Charles Morgan 35, lived here with his wife Elizabeth and 6 children. Charles was a fuller, most likely working at the Town Mill. John Thorne appears in the 1846/50 Church rates, and by the time of the 1851 census George & Fanny Mills, having moved here from No. 8 now had 6 children. In 1861 Enoch Millard 39, working as a labourer in the dyehouse is here with his wife Sophia 39 and 6 children. In 1871 William Ames 42, also a dyehouse labourer, lived here with his wife Hannah 38. No further residents have been traced for the next 50 years. In the Frome directories Frederick Whitmarsh is listed here from 1927-1930, A F Winslow from 1934-1957, Mrs E C R English in 1957, Ralph G Hill from 1961 to 1994, and Gary and Vivienne Lee. It was renovated by its present owner Jeremy Walwin and from 2008 the house has been occupied by Alexander and Karen McNicoll.

11 WILLOW VALE (Weaver's Cottage)

Architecture

This small cottage, which is shown on the 1813 map, is attached to the left of "Dyers". When it was sold recently it was described as having a *"Living Room 12 x 11 ft, Kitchen 12 x 7 ft, with 2 bedrooms above: 15 x 9 ft and 9 x 8 ft."* Its latest owners have done much to enhance its appearance, installing new windows, external shutters, a name plate, and freshening up the paintwork.

Owners & Occupiers

Among the possible occupiers traced are:

1785	John Wise, dyehouseman
1821-1827	William Curtis
1841	Rachael George, 90, and servant
1851	Sarah Thorne 40, laundress, plus James & Rebecca Single 18, printer's apprentice & seamstress.
1861	Sarah Thorne 53 and servant.
1871-1881	George Moon 45, general labourer, and his wife Sarah
1929-1930	Alfred Winslow
1934	Mrs Short and Mrs H MacArthur
1948	Mrs G A V MacArthur
1954	Kenneth F Hobbs

The representatives of the late Frederick Walwin conveyed the property to K F Hobbs (butcher) of 57 Catherine Street for £250 in 1954.

1957	H I Edwards
1960-1961	Mrs I K Stafford.

Mrs Stafford was affected by the 1960 floods. The "Somerset Standard" reported "3 feet of water in the lower rooms, but Mrs Stafford and two of her family went to Trowbridge for the day."

1964-1979	Roger & Mrs Kelly

Roger Kelly subsequently became Director of the Centre for Alternative Technology at Machynlleth in Wales.

1979	T D Denham
2007	Paul & Sheila Mullett

DYERS (former dyehouse workshop)

This plain stone building fronting onto Willow Vale began life as part of the dyehouse. Between 1880 and 1910 it was owned by A R Baily, who had acquired it from John Olive's estate. In 1910 Newport & Sons, who were renting it for £11 per annum acquired it at a sale of Baily's estate. Its single storey had remained derelict for many years after use as a motor vehicle workshop where both Willow Motors and Barnes Coachworks had their origins. It was given Grade II listing in 1983. Recently it was converted into a substantial and ingeniously designed 2-storey residence, appropriately named "Dyers". It is now owned by Geoffrey and Christine Jackson, who are probably the first and only people ever to have lived there. Mr Jackson has reported the existence of a blocked up entrance to a tunnel facing north in the yard at the rear of his house which could have been the entrance to the drying stove's stokehole.

THE WILLOW VALE DYEHOUSE

The major industry in Pilly Vale in the 18th and 19th centuries was the dyeing of wool and woollen cloth. The substantial premises of the dyehouse extended from No. 6 (The Old Kiln) to beyond Willow Vale House. In 1796 the house was advertised for sale by Samuel Allen, together with *"a dyehouse adjoining, comprising 6 blue vats, 5 furnaces for coloured work, a scouring furnace, washing sheds, drying shed, stove, drying yard, store rooms, etc., with two tenements adjoining, and a*

Wool drying stove

stable for 10 beasts". It was purchased by Major John Olive and operated by Sheppards until the mid-1840s, followed by William and Edward Parish, who also ran the dyehouse at Shawford Mill. In its heyday it had 12 vats and 7 furnaces, employing 52 men, a number of whom were resident in Willow Vale. There were a further 7 vats and 4 furnaces at his dyehouse in Justice Lane.

Old Kiln undercroft

The remains of a number of its significant structures can still be seen today. These include a well shaft in the garden of No. 6 which, together with other wells under Riverside Terrace and elsewhere on the site which have since been filled in, would have provided the essential clean water supply. A large cellar or undercroft at No. 6 measuring 14 x 40 feet with a barrel-vaulted stone roof, has a drainage channel running down the centre of the floor. There has been speculation that this could have been used for the fermentation process for manufacturing a blue dye from the woad plant.

The most prominent remaining feature is the circular wool drying stove bordering the garden of No. 6 and the Old Coach House. Now missing its conical roof it is a building worthy of restoration. A similar tower overlooking Market Yard with an art gallery on the first floor is now Frome's Tourist Information Centre. It was essential to dry wool quickly after washing and dyeing. These towers or stoves as they were also known were used for the purpose. They would be of two or three storeys with slatted floors and a central iron stove with a flue carried up to the apex of the roof. The wool would be hung up to dry on a tree-like wooden support with removable branches. Further remains of workshops, dye pits and other buildings on the site would bear archaeological investigation to uncover further evidence of the dyeing of cloth in Frome.

Dyeing the Blues

In the late 18th and early 19th century Frome was an industrious area with a number of dyers' workshops. Some were owned by the dyers themselves; others leased from the clothiers. There appear to be at least 18 dyeing vats possibly used for woad in the various dye works, along with dyeing furnaces for other colours and several drying stove buildings or kilns.

Wool was supplied by local clothiers who would have some of it contracted to be dyed in the wool by specialist blue dyers before it was spun. Fashion trends were as changeable then as now. *"I hope in God all Blues coming round are dark, for I do declare I cannot sell a middling blue. Dark Blues are very much wanted and we must have an assortment."* (correspondence between Elderton, factor, and Noad, cloth maker at Shawford Mill, Beckington from 1763 to 1769).

"Few people at first either can approve of the smell of woad or of a woad vat, though when in condition, they become quite agreeable to those whose business it is to attend them." To give an idea of the scale of the work, a blue vat was 7ft 6in deep with the same diameter at the bottom narrowing to 6ft at the top, holding approximately 1640 ale gallons (2% larger than an imperial gallon). There were widely accepted standards, and if Workshops were well managed, they could expect a blue vat using prime ingredients to colour 220lbs of wool every week. After the last addition of indigo during the 6-week working down period 400lbs of dark blue wool, 200lbs of half blue and 2lbs of very light blue. *"However, there is probably no article more uncertain in its strength and quality than woad. Too much lime in the vat will make the liquor feel slippery and require careful attention to ensure the whole contents of the vat is not irrevocably lost. Too little will make it feel rough and when adding lime the fermentation will come on so swiftly and suddenly that there will be a strong fetid odour arising from putrefactive fermentation and the contents of the vat will again be lost".*

It required considerable practical skill to judge and tend the blue vats. *"A vat of this size is set with 560lbs of the best woad, 5lbs of madder, one peck of* bran, the refuse of wheat, 4 lbs of copperas and a quarter of a peck of slaked lime. Then 15lbs of well ground indigo is added. Over the course of several days carefully attend to it every couple of hours, adjusting ingredients to ensure it ferments correctly. At the end, the liquor will look very rich in the bead, the bubbles will arise of all sizes and will have passed from blue to copper colour. The liquor now when raked up will be a rich yellow with clouds of indigo. When the vat assumes all these appearances it is said to be in fine condition. But, as it often happens, the vat does not come on in a regular way but when the vat has been brought to work, a cross is suspended across it on which the net will rest, about 40lbs of wool is wet in at once. When it is all in it must be handled very briskly the whole time when a vat is new and strong of indigo or the colour will be uneven. In dyeing with woad there should always be two vats in operation at the same time, one

18c Dye Recipe Book from Wallbridge Mill (Bath Central Library)

that has been worked for one or two months and a new one. Wool should be primed in the new one and finished in the older one. A vat that is set with 500lbs of woad will require 500lbs more during the working, this will colour for 6 months, in that time it will take nearly 500lbs of indigo. After each *dyeing the vat must be attended and renewed. It is usual in all regular dye-houses to reheat on Saturdays in the afternoon and again on Tuesdays or Wednesdays according to the vat works".*

After the wool was dyed and washed, blues and blacks were washed away from other colours and dried in the drying stove before it was returned to the clothier. The mixed colours were rolled, teased, carded and scribbled into blends, then spun and woven into different cloths including medleys. Frome's blue dyed cloth was also used for military uniforms, particularly during the Napoleonic wars. Blue could also be dyed in the furnace using logwood, alum, cream of tartar and muriate of tin. This colour was of a beautiful dark blue and stood the exposure to the weather for more than a month, but in another month some parts were changed to a dirty brown. Above all dyers strove to produce consistent results.

The Supply of Woad

Woad (Isatis Tinctoria) is the European indigo bearing plant from the brassica family. It was used to dye wool a range of blues from pale to dark but the concentration of indigo in each plant is small and variable, so from the mid-1500s it was no longer used on its own but with indigo (Indigofera Tinctoria from Asia) in large-scale fermenting vats. The ingredient required from these plants is the chemical indigotin, which is insoluble in water. It needs to be changed by reduction in an alkaline solution to "indigo white" which is soluble. Then, when the wool is immersed in the vat, the fibres absorb the soluble "indigo white" and when it is taken out again and exposed to the air it changes back to blue indigotin – magic! Wool was generally "woaded" before being dyed a darker colour as this would enhance it and make it more lightfast. This is shown in a local dye recipe book from Wallbridge Mill used around the mid 1700s which shows swatches of woaded wool over-dyed to match a large range of colours.

Woad to supply the vats was imported or possibly grown locally on the Oad Ground in the Trinity area. John Parish, late of Shawford Mill in Beckington, had an article published by the Bath & West Society in 1810 on how best to grow woad. *"I have been many years a considerable consumer of woad, and have also cultivated it with much success. In very wet seasons, woad from poor land is of very little value. I once had occasion to purchase at such time and found that there was no possibility of regulating my vats in their fermentation and I was under the necessity of making every possible effort to obtain some that was the produce of a more congenial season. At this time several dyers experienced much difficulty and one of eminence in the blue trade suffered so much by woad of his own growth that he declared his resolution to decline the trade altogether.*

I now proceed to say something on its preparation for the use of the dyer. Woad when gathered is carried to the mill and ground. These mills grind the leaves small and then they are cast into heaps where they ferment for a fortnight, being occasionally turned, and gain an adhesive consistence and have less juices to squeeze out in balling. The balls must be as compact as possible and placed on hurdles in a shed with air between to dry for a month or more. The immediate use of new woad from the couch is not advised by dyers who are experienced, for new woad is not so regular in its fermentation in the blue vat."

THE OLD COACH HOUSE

Architecture & Industry

With its extensive gardens The Old Coach House was once an ancillary building to Willow Vale House. Approached via a driveway between Nos. 11 and 12 the plot stretches northwards to the railway line and includes a large lawn, formerly a tennis court. It was purchased and converted into a dwelling by Harry Wild and his son Basil. Basil and his wife Veronica were the owners in 2010.

Within its grounds are the remains of an elaborate 2-storey gazebo. Basil writes *"The old gazebo at the top of the garden was badly damaged in the great storm of 1987 when the roof blew off, taking with it some masonry. This roof was beautifully constructed with bentwood joists made of elm and* a slate tiled roof. It had a lead weather vane atop, some of which has been preserved. The floor of the interior was made of wide elm boards in a herringbone design. Following the loss of the roof the floor quickly deteriorated and eventually fell in to the lower floor. Following enquiries, Mendip District Council was unable to contribute enough funding to preserve the building, and it continues increasingly rapidly to deteriorate."

An interesting story is told by Basil Wild who relates that: *"When we were securing a retaining wall in one of the outbuildings we found some large bones that turned out to be a fairly intact skeleton of a large shire horse. We put the bones that had fallen out back in place and built the retaining wall against the earth that held them in place."* The mystery was explained later when a man, who was brought up at 12 Willow Vale in the 1930s made contact to see where he lived as a boy. He explained that his *"Dad had been a well known market gardener and Frome strong man, complete with leopard skin and dumbbells."* He said *"He was quite a gentle man compared to their mother, who would think nothing of beating the two boys with iron bars when discipline was necessary. He used the hothouses which went right along the left hand side of the garden to grow fresh fruit and vegetables. Each week his friend, who lived on the outskirts of Frome, would pick up farm produce for the market, and his last stop would be to pick up the produce from Willow Vale. He had a horse and a flat cart that the children loved. Early in the morning they would load their produce, and at the end of the day, Dad would return with his friend. They would park the horse with a nose bag, and promptly go off and get plastered. But one night they got back to Willow Vale to find the horse lying on the road, dead. Being the strong man he was, a hole was dug beside one of the hothouses, and the horse carried up the garden and ceremoniously laid to rest".*

The visitor also told the Wilds that his brother was beaten for *"going under the river"* in the tunnel which was entered from the top of the garden. He said *"This tunnel was perfectly formed, went down about 60 feet, and had steps on the side, and a tunnel that took you across to St John's Church".* He swore that this was all true. The mystery of Frome's tunnels is being investigated by a group of enthusiasts known as the Frome Tunnels Project. Recently they were able to confirm the existence of the steps, but blockage of the tunnel prevented confirmation that it headed towards the church. What seems more likely is that it was part of the dyeworks, and joined the tunnel mentioned by Geoffrey Jackson (See "Dyers").

12 WILLOW VALE

The house abuts the west side of Willow Vale House, and was built in the mid-1930s for Sir John Harris to a design by a local architect Percy Rigg, who also designed Riverside Terrace, which it matches in style.

The first tenant was a P Tuffs (1936-7). No directories were published during the war, and the next tenant recorded is A W Pinkard (1948-1974), a supply teacher at Selwood School. He left for another post in Cornwall, but his mother continued living here. Peter and Veronica Jeffries were in residence in 1978. Since 1981 Lindsey Fowler has occupied the house with her daughter Leah.

WILLOW VALE HOUSE

Architecture

The land on which Willow Vale House was built formed part of the endowment of the medieval Chantry of Our Lady in St. John's Church, Frome, which also included much of the Trinity area and elsewhere. By the 17th century it had become the property of the Smith family of Combe Hay near Bath. Robert Smith built Rook Lane House in 1690 and lived there until his death in 1703.

In 1796 it was advertised for sale by Samuel Allen as *"That very good dwellinghouse on the verge of the Frome containing 2 parlours, kitchen, lodging rooms and regular suite of offices with 2 exceedingly pleasant gardens, the walls of which are stocked with fruit trees."* The purchaser was Major John Olive. He was rated at 1/7d for his house and stable, and 8/1d for other property in Willow Vale. In 1816 he added a wing to the right of the main house which in the 1930s was to become a separate dwelling known as "The Willows".

When the property was auctioned in 1933 it was described as a *"Detached freehold residence with good gardens, greenhouses, tennis court and garage, in a delightful situation facing south, secluded and off the main road. The house is substantially built of stone with tiled roof, and contains: 2 reception rooms, lounge hall, principal and back staircases, large kitchen, pantry, larder, scullery, coal house, 4 principal bedrooms, 2 attic bedrooms, bathroom (h. & c.), lavatory, etc. Electric light, gas and water laid on. The gardens are nicely laid out and include flower and fruit gardens, 3 greenhouses, and a grass tennis court. Adjoining is a set of well-built stabling, having a frontage of about 100 ft to Willow Vale, and garden at the back to a depth of about 114 ft., this forming an ideal building site. All that capital walled-in garden at the north side of Willow Vale House, lying facing south extending to an area of about 1 acre, including buildings of pig sty and round house. This lot has a 9ft. wide entrance from Willow Vale through the adjoining yard, and forms an excellent building plot or market garden".* Willow Vale House and The Willows were first awarded Grade II listed building status in 1949.

Owners & Occupiers

The Smith and Allen families   In 1724 Margaret Smith, widow, and her son Robert Smith leased to Henry Allen of Frome the dyehouse, built by his father Henry Allen, a 2-acre close of meadow called Lower Pilly Close, and another close of meadow called Gurlover of 1 acre, paying 4 guineas a year rent for the usual 99 years and 3 lives. This was renewed in 1733 to Mary Allen, and again in 1734, including the messuage lately built by Mary Allen, thus dating the house and its builder. The house was later sold to her son Edward Allen for £200.

When Robert's grandson John Smith died, he left debts amounting to £18,000 and the Smith Estate Act was passed to enable trustees to sell his property in Frome and elsewhere to pay off these debts. This enabled the Allens to buy the freehold in 1776. The 1785 census shows Henry Allen the younger in residence with two females and one other male. In 1796 Willow Vale House and the dyehouse were put up for sale by Samuel Allen, dyer, and purchased by Major John Olive, along with several other properties in the Vale.

The Olive Family   Having acquired the property in 1796 Major Olive lived here until his death on 23rd December 1826. The 1827 rates list his rateable property as:

Tenant	Owner	Property	House No.	Rate
T. Brown	late John Olive	House	(No. 4)	7½d
Wm. Carter	late John Olive	House	(No. 4a)	2d
Messrs. Sheppard	late John Olive	Wool warehouse, stove, drying house, picking shop, stable, etc. (Surrounding Nos. 4 & 5)		2/2½d
(At some stage Olive had acquired Frome Town Mill from the Earl of Cork)				
I. Fisher	late John Olive	House	(No. 5)	6¼d
Kemp	late John Olive	House	(No. 6)	5d
Benjamin George	late John Olive	House	(No. 7)	2d
James Budd	late John Olive	House	(No. 8b)	0¾d
James Macey	late John Olive	House	(No. 8)	1½d

Messrs. Sheppard	late John Olive	Shops	(No. 9)	2¼d
John Olive (V)	late John Olive	House, Cellar, etc.	(No. 10)	3d
William Curtis	late John Olive	House	(No. 11)	0¾d
John Olive (V)	John Olive	Dyehouse, premises		1/8¼d
Charles Richards	John Olive	House	(No. ?)	1½d
John Olive	John Olive	House, stable, etc. (W.V.H.)		1/9d
John Olive	John Olive	Gardens (Willow Vale House)		7½d
William Joyce	John Olive	House	(No. ?)	2¾d

Note: Current house numbers, shown in brackets, have been added.

John's widow Elizabeth (Betty) Olive continued living here until her own death on 23rd March 1847. She appears in the 1841 census aged 75, with Fanny Shingles 15, and servant Elizabeth Padfield 21. John and Betty's memorial is inside St John's Church, above the door to the parvise room. Their only daughter died in infancy, and the property was inherited by John's nephew, John Olive V (1799-1865). A landed proprietor from Chippenham, Alfred Taylor 54 was in occupation with his wife Sarah, elder brother and a servant according to the 1851 census. Then John and his wife Eliza came to live here. The 1861 census lists Eliza (then aged 50), a servant and visitor, but John may have been away at the time. They continued living here until his death on 14th May 1865. 15 years were to pass before his estate was sold. Harding & Sons arranged the auction on 2nd June 1880, which included:

Lot 2   Capital residence at Pilly Hill in occupation of Edmund Baily (Willow Vale House, purchased by A R Baily).

Lot 3   Ruinous building known as the Town Mill with hatches, washing stand, and iron Waterwheel (purchased by A R Baily).

Lot 4   Blocks of buildings, Dyehouse, stables, large yards, Drying Ground, and well constructed and newly built Shaft and also newly built Stores and Counting House. (Purchased by Messrs Sheppard and Watson).

Lot 5   Garden Ground of 2 roods, 21 perches, the property of Edmund Olive (purchased by A R Baily).

Lot 6   Substantial dwellinghouse in occupation of Mr Bryant as tenant with right of way for horses, carts and carriages (No. 5, bought in).

Lot 7   Newly erected and well built dwelling house with: Counting House, Stable, Workshops, Sawpit, and Timber Yard in rear in occupation of Mr Brown as tenant (No. 4 purchased by A R Baily). *Also substantially built Factory and Store adjoining, now in occupation of Messrs. Cockey* (purchased by A R Baily)

The Baily Family (See also 3 Willow Vale)   Edmund Baily, an innkeeper and maltster born c1813, was a son of William Baily of the Swan Brewery, which later became part of the Frome United Brewery. By his wife Eliza he had 6 children and in 1839 he is living at the Bath Arms in Palmer Street. He appears there in the 1851 census with his wife, daughter, three sons and servants. He was still licensee in 1866 but had become the tenant of Willow Vale House. He acquired the maltings at 3 Willow Vale in 1868 and installed his son Alfred as maltster. In 1871 he is living here with his wife Eliza, daughter Fanny, and son Charles, a wine merchant. Edmund died in 1880 aged 67 having been in *"declining health for a considerable time"*. He had been churchwarden at St. John's between 1865 and 1880. An inventory and valuation of his personal estate, household furniture and effects was made on 8th September 1880 which totalled £364.7s. His wife Eliza died at Oriel Lodge in Gentle Street on 18th May 1883 aged 69 after a *"long painful illness"*.

Alfred Richard Baily, the second son of Edmund and Eliza, was born c1845. A miller and maltster, from 1868 he ran the maltings at No. 3 Willow Vale and lived in the Malthouse with his family. Following his father's death, in 1880 he purchased Willow Vale House from the Olive's estate and is listed here in the 1881 census aged 36, together with his wife Mary Susanna, their daughter Ethel, and 2 servants. Alfred purchased a plantation adjoining Willow Vale House for £72.19s in December 1886. Together with his brother they founded Messrs E Baily & Sons Ltd at the new Station Maltings and in 1905, purchased the Frome Vinegar Works at Welshmill for £905.

In December 1899 he sold Willow Vale House and the plantation and moved to North End, Bridge Street. Mary died at North End aged 59 on 13th May 1903, and Alfred, under tragic circumstances when a fire broke out in the house on 28th January 1910. Later that year the residue of his estate in

Willow Vale was auctioned, including: No 2 Willow Vale, a storehouse ("Dyers") and the Town Mill site. Alfred's daughter Mary later bequeathed the Mary Baily Playing Field to the National Playing Fields Association.

Mrs Maria Elizabeth Ormerod widow of the Rev. Charles Ormerod , a vicar from Croydon, purchased the house from Alfred Baily in 1899 for £1,100 and remained here until her death on 7th September 1910. According to the Frome Almanac, Colonel G Osborne was tenant in 1912. In January 1919 Mrs Ormerod's daughter sold the house for £750 to Edward and Bessie Powney. Edward was a pork butcher at 20 Catherine Hill. They lived here until August 1934 when they sold the property to Sir John Harris. The Powneys moved to Hall House in Cork Street, and then to 7 Trinity Parade. Edward died in the Victoria Hospital on 15th December 1955 at the age of 84. The previous August he and his wife had celebrated their diamond wedding anniversary. Bessie died at Rowden House on 9th February 1963, aged 96. Both were buried in Holy Trinity churchyard.

Sir John Hobbis Harris

Sir John was a retired Colonial Administrator living at "Stonelands" in Bath Road, Frome. He had married Alice Seeley from Frome on 6 May 1898. They had two sons and two daughters. He later moved to Dorking in Surrey. In 1934 he purchased the freehold of Willow Vale House and the adjoining land for £900 as an investment. He commissioned local architects Rigg & Vallis of Monmouth House to draw up plans to make the 1816 wing into a self-contained residence (The Willows); for a house to be attached to the left side of Willow Vale House (No. 12); and to design a terrace of 5 houses (Riverside Terrace) to replace the stables to the right.

Sir John returned to Frome and died at "Stonelands" on 30th April 1940. Under the terms of his will 10% of the income from his investments was to go to the Anti-Slavery and Aborigines Protection Society following the death of his wife. This would have included the rents and sale values of his properties in Willow Vale.

In 1936 S Moody was Sir John's tenant, but around 1937 Hedley Joseph Pudden moved to Willow Vale House. A native of Castle Cary, in his early days he was engaged in the grocery trade. After a long period of business there he came to Frome to manage Messrs Giddings Stores in Vallis Way, a business which he took over after a few weeks. In 1932 he was appointed as Frome's Librarian and continued as such until Christmas 1950 when he retired after 18 years service. He was formerly a lay preacher at the Wesley Methodist Church, and ran a 40 strong bible class there for many years. He was keenly interested in local history, particularly that of Methodism in Frome, and was a frequent lecturer.

Mrs Vera Hazel Wordell purchased the house in March 1953 for £1,150. Her husband, Robert Anthony Wordell, was a tobacconist at 14 Market Place. They lived here until 1959 when Mrs Wordell sold it for £2,350 to Mrs Joyce Elizabeth Lloyd, the wife of Dr Lloyd who had previously lived in part of Marston House. During the 1960 flood Mrs Lloyd had water in her kitchen and scullery. Michael and Mary Hemmett were the next owners, living here from 1966 to 1975. They were followed by Brian and Helen Nash, who lived here from 1975 to 1982. Brian worked for Butler & Tanner and Helen was involved in organising playgroups and Frome Town Council. She became Frome's first Lady Mayor. They moved to Wales, but following Brian's death Helen moved back to live in Warminster. Jo and Sue Teller bought the house in February 1983 and lived there until early 1996 when they returned to London. Peter and Veronica Birch purchased the property in 1996.

The Willows

This extension to the right of Willow Vale House was built in 1816. For its earlier history and ownership see Willow Vale House. It became a separate residence in 1935, soon after its purchase by Sir John Harris. The rear garden was divided in a most strange way with the large house not having ownership, but the newly built No. 12 having most of the land. R F Green occupied The Willows as tenant from 1936 to 1955. Raymond and Angela Daniel purchased the property from Mrs Ashworth, daughter of Sir John Harris, in October 1959 for £500 and have lived in the house for over 50 years.

Nos. 1 – 5 RIVERSIDE TERRACE

Architecture

Sir John Harris commissioned a local architect, Percy Rigg, to draw up plans for a terrace of 5 houses on the site of the former stables to the right of The Willows. We are fortunate to have a copy of his original drawings for the front elevation and plan. The stables were demolished, a well covered over, and the terrace was built in 1934/5. At first it was to be called "Riverside Cottages" then "Drive" before "Riverside Terrace" was finally settled on.

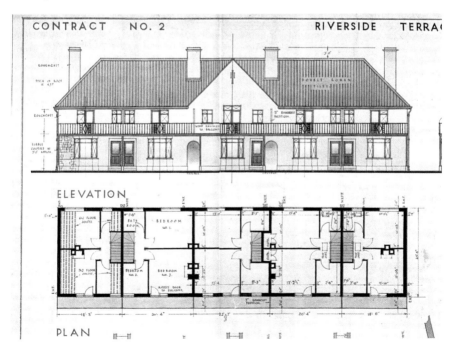

A typical layout of the individual houses comprised a hall, sitting room, kitchen/dining room and pantry with external toilet on the ground floor, with 3 bedrooms and bathroom on the first floor. Over the years owners have improved the houses. Internal access to the downstairs lavatories was created from the kitchen via the pantry. The collective agreement of owners to replace a variety of dilapidated balcony fencing to an attractive standard design has greatly enhanced the overall appearance of the terrace. A number have recently added rear extensions to enlarge kitchens or conservatories, which involved excavating into the steep hillside. Some have extended into the roof space to provide a further bedroom. No. 5 has been completely re-modelled internally. Where space was sufficient, garages or parking spaces have been built on the river bank opposite.

Owners and Occupiers

The initial tenants and gross monthly rents were:

No. 1	T Coles	£3.13.8d	No. 2	Mr Nash	£3.13.8d
No. 3	L O Browning	£4.00.0d	No. 4	Mr Hewitt	£3.13.8d
No. 5	Miss Lincoln	£3.13.8d			

No. 1 was sold to Eric James & Rachel Wilson in June 1967. No. 2 was sold to N G & R A Rose in 1972 for £3,800, and then to Edith Irene Gill in 1978. Between the mid-1960s and early 1990s prices averaged around £50,000, but in line with the housing market generally prices rose rapidly over the next decade to around the £200,000 mark. In 2009 the owners were: No. 1 Angela Osborne, No. 3 Alison & Peter Francis, No. 4 Carolyn Griffiths & Jonathan Stearn, and No. 5 Eva and Dan Lupton. No. 2 was sold by Steve Jenkins and Gary Hopkins in July 2009.

THE QUEEN ANNE TERRACE (14-17 Willow Vale)

This fine Queen Anne style terrace stands at the eastern end of Willow Vale. It was built on land at Pilly Hill which in medieval times belonged to the Chantry Chapel of Our Lady in St John's Church. This had been founded in 1314 and was dissolved in 1548. Robert Smith, the clothier, who built and lived in Rook Lane House, bought lands belonging to the former Chantry in 1607, and on 6th August 1609 leased an acre of those lands on Pilly Hill to a Christopher Smith (perhaps a relation) for 1,000 years at an annual rent of 21/4d. This lease, or quit rent, passed through Christopher's descendants until 1745, as follows:

Christopher Smith	*1609 to 1636*
Thomas Smith, his son	*1636 to 1657*

Michael Smith, son of Thomas	1657 to 1702
Henry Smith, nephew of Michael	1702 to 1711
James Smith, son of Henry	1711 to his death (not traced)
Ann, daughter of Henry and wife of Edward Mortimer of Trowbridge	1711-?

Ann Mortimer, daughter and heir of Ann and Edward who, shortly after sold it to Josiah Ames the elder, clothier of Frome, on 25th March 1745.

The terrace is first mentioned in the Church Rates of 1723, when James Smith is rated for *"2 houses at Pilly Hill, or occupiers 6d"*. Previously the Smith family had been rated the same 6d for *"1 acre on Pilly Hill"*. It is very possible that the houses were built between 1711 when James Smith inherited and 1723, although rate collectors continued to use the previous description.

Throughout the 18th century only two houses are mentioned in the rates. The occupants were clothiers, so that workshops were a necessary part of the facilities they needed. One would have been the present No. 14, together with the adjoining cottage, and with a side entrance to the basement. The other was the rest of the terrace; now Nos. 15 to 17. The fact that the back garden of No. 15 stretches the whole width of the two houses, and the possibility that there is a blocked doorway at the back of the pantry on the ground floor, and another at the end of the first floor corridor is further evidence of 15 and 16 being one house. When 16 was made into a separate house the canopy from No. 15 may have been moved when a window was changed to create a front door for No. 16, and a new one put in its place. Changes in the stonework can be seen.

In addition, rates list workshops with this property which extended beyond where the railway line now runs. When the Radstock to Frome line was planned the Great Western Railway Company bought the workshop at the end of the terrace, demolished what was necessary to construct the line, and sold the rest, which became the cottage at No. 17. The side of this has a blocked doorway and window a few feet from the track.

Opposite the terrace, the gardens on the riverbank formed part of a field belonging to the Longleat Estate until 1886, and did not become gardens until 1900. The road at this end of the Vale has not been adopted by the Local Authority, and both the road and riverbank are owned by householders.

In the schedule to the Smith Estate act of 1776, passed to enable John Smith's executors to pay his extensive debts of over £18,000, Josiah Ames is listed as holding the lease and still paying the 21s 4d quit rent. Shortly after, Josiah must have bought the lease itself, and so merged it into the freehold of the property. Josiah died in 1772 and left Nos. 15-17, as now numbered, to his elder son Josiah Ames junior, and No. 14 to his other son James. The latter, however, died in 1773 without an heir, and his brother inherited his share as well.

Josiah junior died in 1802 without issue and left all his property, including freehold property in Willow Vale to his wife Ann. She died in 1803, leaving her property to trustees to sell and pay bequests to 43 people, ranging from £5 to £500, and totalling £4,485. In addition, the acre of land in Pilly Vale with the two houses was sold to a local solicitor, James Anthony Wickham of North Hill House in 1804 for a total of £1,120. It was soon after this transaction that the two houses were converted into three (Nos. 14 to 16). Wickham died in 1854, leaving his estates to his eldest son James Whalley Dawe Thomas Wickham. The latter died in 1885 and his estate was sold on 6th October the following year. Now for the first time the various houses in the terrace passed into separate ownership, in some instances to the occupiers:-

Lot 6 No. 7 (now No. 14) was sold for £400 to Edmund Olive
Lot 7 No. 8 (now No. 15) sold after auction for £200 to Walter Harrold
Lot 9 No. 9 (now No. 16) was bought in at £250
Lot 10 No. 10 (now No. 17) was bought in at £220

Nos. 16 and 17 were eventually acquired by George Alfred Daniel. For further details of ownership and occupancy see the sections covering the individual properties below.

The terrace was first awarded Grade II* Listed Building status in 1949. It is currently described as: "Terrace of 3 circa 1720 clothiers' houses, No 16 *probably a later addition. Coursed rubble with freestone dressings, pantile roofs, dormers, stone stacks with capping. Moulded plinth, moulded eaves cornice. 2 storeys and attics (3+3+2 gabled dormers) and cellars. Windows spaced 5+5+3, sashes in bolection architraves with cornices and pulvinated friezes to ground floor windows. Central (No 16 to left) panelled doors under hollow semi-circular hoods on scrolled brackets, bolection architraves to door openings. Return of No 14 has blocked narrow openings and a 2 storey mullion window and a single light window on ground floor with moulded surrounds and drips. Rear: No's 14 and 15 have stair turrets with bolection surrounds to glazing bar sashes, on ground floors a small sash window with edge roll and cornice. No 15 has stepped chimney to rear extension. No 16 has a 2-light ogee mullion window on the 1st floor. No's 14 and 15 interiors: good staircase with heavy moulded handrail, straight string and squat balusters (No 15 has ball newels). No 15 has stop-moulded ovolo door surrounds. On 1st floor west room of No 15 is a bolection surround fireplace with inserted egg-timer grate. No 15 has a double pile segmental barrel vaulted cellar adjoining the kitchen."*

14 WILLOW VALE

Architecture

The house is first mentioned in the Church Rates of 1723 when James Smith was the owner, but could have been built at any time between 1711 and then. The earliest description we have is from when it was auctioned as Lot 7 of James Wickham's estate on 6th October 1886. It was purchased by solicitor Edmund Olive, who sold it at auction on 7th August 1889, described as: *"Freehold family dwellinghouse with gardens and 2 conservatories at the back and a lawn in front with side entrance, in occupation of the owner. The house contains a large dry cellar, 3 sitting rooms, china pantry, kitchen, scullery, larder, 4 bedrooms, 3 attics, w.c. and a noble oak staircase* (elm in fact). *The doorway from the back garden to the plantation and the side entrance to Mr Baily's property will be walled up by the vendor before completion"*. Over its 300 year history there have been many changes to the layout and details of the house. Nevertheless it retains perhaps more of its original features than any other house in Willow Vale and has been carefully and sympathetically restored by its present owner, John Cheetham.

Owners and Occupiers

The first occupiers, identified in the 1724 rates, are Henry and Mary Allen. Henry had founded the dyehouse in Willow Vale but was dead by 1734 when his wife acted as his executrix. By 1741 she had built Willow Vale House for her own use and presumably moved there from 14 Willow Vale. A Mrs Moore is named as tenant in the will dated 12th September 1771 of Josiah Ames. He had acquired the terrace in 1745 from a descendant of the Smith family. Michael Burrell (gent.) is listed as occupier in the 1785 survey. He was a solicitor and brother-in-law of Josiah Ames the elder, having

married Martha Ames in 1731. He had no direct heirs of his own and in his will dated 4th November 1791 he left a legacy to his great nephew Josiah Ames, who died 2 years later, and the residue to Josiah Ames junior, his nephew, and the latter's wife Ann. The will was proved at the Prerogative Court of Canterbury in January 1792. The 1810 rates list Ralph Hotchkin as occupier.

William Davis is listed as occupier in the rates between 1818 and 1838. Born on 14th July 1783, William was a Magistrates' clerk for 17 years, as well as Vestry Clerk and Returning Officer for the Borough of Frome and a qualified attorney. He died on 1st November 1848 aged 65, and was buried at the east end of St John's churchyard, beside the grave of Bishop Ken. A window in the south wall of the Church tower is in his memory. His wife, Mary Ann, was a poet. A number of her poems were published in the *"Selwood Wreath"*; a collection of local poems edited by Charles Bayly, of which there is a copy in Frome Museum. She also wrote a hymn for the Dedication of

Holy Trinity Church in 1838. Mary came from Middlesex and is listed in the 1851 census as living here aged 68, with 3 middle-aged servants: Charles Holdeway, and Lucy and Anna Maidment, and again in the 1861 census, but with only 2 servants. Mary died at Bideford in Devon on 19th March 1874, aged 91, and was buried in her husband's grave in Frome. She has a memorial brass beneath the window under the tower of St John's Church. Mary Davis's poem, "Song" from the *"Selwood Wreath"* is reproduced below.

Butterfly, with wings of gold,
Bend thy burnished pinions hither,
Ere blossoms which I behold,
In the scorching sunbeams wither.
Come fair insect and repose,
All thy fears to silence hushing,
On this velvet-blossom'd rose,
Fresh and fragrant, lovely, blushing.

Whither dost thou speed thy flight,
Giddy and incautious stranger?
Shun the bow'r that blooms so bright –
Shun the bow'r – 'tis fraught with danger!
There, to lure thee as his prey,
Underneath its branches lurking,
See! A bullfinch marks thy way:
Ruin in his breast is working.

Life, like thee, is on the wing;
All its joys are fast declining;
Seize its pleasures as they spring,
When with innocence combining.
Come, fair insect, and repose,
All thy fears to silence hushing,
On this velvet-blossom'd rose,
Fresh and fragrant, lovely, blushing.

In the 1871 census George Alfred Daniel of Frome, age 32 is in residence with his wife Isabella from Newport, Monmouthshire, their four daughters aged from 3 years to 2 months, and 3 servants. George's brother Charles Henry Daniel, a clerk in Holy Orders at Wareham was also staying with them at the time. Dr Frederick Joshua Parsons, MRCS, born about 1849, had moved here in 1881 from his previous home at North End, 14 Bridge Street. His father, Dr Joshua Parsons, was family physician to the Kent family, and was therefore a witness at the Road Hill House inquest and murder trial in 1860. This was a "cause célèbre" and has been investigated by many, including Charles Dickens. The story is recounted in great detail in Kate Summerscale's *"The Suspicions of Mr Whicher"*. Dr Parsons was still living here in 1886 when the terrace was auctioned. He married Alice Maria, and had two sons, both born in Pilly Vale. By 1907 he had moved to Garston House where he died on 2nd February 1912 at the age of 62. Two of his brothers were also doctors. Another brother, Alfred Parsons RA (1847-1920), born at Beckington, became a world famous painter, illustrator, landscape architect and garden designer, and member of the Royal Academy.

Edmund Olive, the elder son of Edmund and Eliza Olive, was born on 6th July 1847. He was articled in the offices of Messrs. Cruttwell & Co. in Bath Street, Frome. On being admitted as a solicitor he moved briefly to London. The 1887-1890 directories list him practising at Bridge Street, but he seems to have succeeded Dr Parsons at 14 Willow Vale, which he purchased as Lot 6 for £400 from the Wickham family on 21st December 1886, and came to live here soon after. He served in the Volunteer Movement, becoming Lieutenant in the Frome Camp. He was not here for long as his estate was auctioned on 7th August 1889, but the auction failed to find a buyer (see description under "Architecture"). Edmund then went to Dominica as a fruit farmer until he contracted malaria, from which he suffered for the rest of his life. He returned to live at 6 Kingland Place, Poole, where he died of heart failure on 25th February 1905, aged 58. He was buried in his parents' family vault in St John's churchyard. Edmund married Harriet Ellen and had 4 children. Following his death she moved to Bath and died on 16th December 1916 at 1 Pier Terrace, West Bath, where she had lived for 7 years. She too was buried in St John's churchyard.

Andrew Whitehead from Twerton is listed as occupier in the 1891 census with his wife Alice Elizabeth and a servant. He is also recorded in the 1890 and 1892 directories, but is not mentioned the following year. According to the Frome Directory, Richard Harding is living here in 1894. This could be either the second son of Charles Harding senior, born at Woolverton, Somerset c1820, who was an auctioneer in the family firm and living at Rodden Lake in 1892, but stayed only briefly, for his household furniture and effects were auctioned on 1st October 1895. Or alternatively he was the son of Richard Harding, estate agent, and builder of Critchill House. If so he was a farmer, based there in 1886, and agent for the Royal Farmers' Fire Life Insurance Company. By 1883 he had moved to 2 Wallbridge and by 1889 to Styles Hill, where he was agent for the Alliance Fire and Life Insurance Company. He married Elizabeth Sangar, who was born in Bristol, and had issue: Herbert 1864, Bertha c1866, Agnes c1869, Douglas c1871, and Constance c1873. Thomas Edwards is listed here in directories between 1898 and 1905. He was an insurance agent for the Wesleyan & General, London & Counties, and Plate Glass insurance companies. By 1906 he was living at 2 Alexandra Terrace in Frome.

Charles John Grant was a member of the family which ran their painting and decorating business from, and later occupied No. 4 Willow Vale. Having lived at No. 5 from 1889-1894 he is listed as living here at No. 14 in local directories from 1907-1926. His brothers Harold and Douglas James Grant are also listed at this address in the 1910 voters list. In 1916 the house was valued at £200. Charles had married Emma, who died here on 8th February 1920, aged 74. Their youngest son Graham was wounded in France and died in Cheltenham Hospital on 6th February 1916.

Mrs A Charlton is listed here only in the 1927 directory, and was probably living at 11 Redland Terrace by 1930. Miss Ann Elizabeth Thompson and Miss Rosaleen Tessy Smallbone-Masters are listed in the 1929 directory. Miss Masters came to Frome in about 1926 and lived with Miss Thompson as her companion. When Miss Thompson died aged 97 in 1949 Miss Masters continued to live here until her own death in 1956 at the age of 84. Following Miss Master's death, William and Winifred Codrington purchased the property. As a widow, Mrs Codrington died in 1996 when John Cheetham, acquired both 14a and 14 Willow Vale.

14a WILLOW VALE (The Cottage)

Architecture

This small cottage is attached to the left of No. 14. The owner of both 14 and 14a, John Cheetham writes: *"The 1813 Cruse map shows a building where this property stands, presumably not a dwelling but a workshop. The two properties, 14 and 14a should probably be assessed architecturally together, at least since 1813. The ground floor interconnecting door between the two is, essentially due to its detailing, an exterior door to No. 14. Therefore the property known as 14a seems likely to*  *have been an addition using much older reclaimed material. The rear window to the main bedroom of No. 14 is now blocked up and within the roof space of No. 14a. As a whole there is clear evidence of two, possibly three kitchens. The first in the basement of No. 14, the existing one in No. 14a, and possibly a third in the large ground floor room in No. 14, where there was almost certainly a much larger 'inglenook' or fireplace range with side access to ovens."*

The auction details of 1889 describe No. 14 as having 3 sitting rooms, which could mean that either the large ground floor of No. 14a had reverted to that use by then, or that the large room over it was a sitting room as it had access at first floor level to the garden.

Owners and Occupiers (see also No. 14)

D Purchase was living here in 1948, and from 1949 to 1955 Wilfred Frank Spalding. Born in 1920 he left Frome to seek ordination in Sarum and was ordained a deacon in 1957 and priest in 1958. From 1969 to 1985 he was Rector of Hoole in the Blackburn diocese, but retired to Fulwood in Preston.

His wife Jean was the daughter of a nurseryman in Locks Hill. A cellist, Miss F Gibson, is listed as living here in 1960/61 with her sister.

A remarkable man, Angus C M Maitland is listed here from 1970 to 1986. He had been a tea planter in Sri Lanka, descended from the Earls of Lauderdale, who enjoyed visiting his Scottish relations. He was also a motor bike enthusiast, winning many cups, and did not give up riding until his late 80s. He had previously owned and lived in Beckington Castle, but sold it to buy 14a Willow Vale where he lived until he died in his 90s. Paul A Kidelan purchased the cottage from Maitland's executors, renovated and lived in it until after his marriage, when he moved to Rodden Down. Derek Wilkinson was tenant during 1996-7 when it was purchased by John Cheetham, who reunited it with No. 14 in February 1999 by reopening the doors linking through.

15 WILLOW VALE

This central part of the terrace was formerly linked to No. 16 and the adjoining workshop (now No. 17), which were collectively rated at 3d during the 18th century. The first occupier to be traced is a Mrs Weaver, whose name is mentioned in the 1742 rates. Clothier Peter Chapman is first listed in the 1742 rates and in the assignment of the lease dated 25th March 1745. He seems to have moved from Willow Vale to Garston House, which he purchased in October 1774 for £300 freehold. His will is dated

1765 and that of his wife Silvestris (nee Clavey) were both proved in February 1768. There is a memorial to them in St John's Church.

Josiah Ames the elder (1701-1772) was assigned the 1,000 year lease by Ann Mortimer on 25th March 1745, and was in residence from soon after until his death in 1772. In 1731 he married Martha Burrell and had 6 children, of whom 3 died in infancy. Only Josiah's third son, Josiah Ames junior (1738-1802), survived him. He was also a clothier, and spent most of his life in Willow Vale. When he died in September 1802 his wife Ann inherited his entire estate, their only son Josiah having died aged only 19 in 1793. However, she died a month later, and with no direct heirs, left bequests to many people, mostly in Frome, totalling £4,485. In 1804 Anne's trustees sold the terrace to James Anthony Wickham and a succession of tenants lived in the houses. A Mrs Prosser is listed in the 1810 rates and T Daniel *(the late)* in 1818.

Harry Cruse is listed in the rates from 1820 to 1838 when he was assessed for 7½d. He and his wife died within a year of each other at a very young age: his wife on 10th January 1843 aged 28 and Harry on 7th January 1844 aged 29. He had been Parish clerk at St John's. The 1841 census lists Henrietta Cruse 35, schoolmistress, Charlotte 60, Elizabeth 30, teacher, Mary 25 and Louisa 15, plus a servant and 6 pupils. The *"Bath Chronicle"* of 16th July 1840 contained the following advertisement.

> **Miss & Mrs Cruse's Preparatory School (at Willow Vale)**
> **for Young Gentlemen under ten years of age**
> **will re-open on Monday next, 20th July.**
> **References given (if required) to Clergy**
> **and the Parents of Pupils.**

Sarah Miles, born in Frome, is listed here in the 1846/1850 rates and the 1851 census, when she was a widow, living here alone aged 54. In the 1861 census Alfred 40 and Ann 41 Haynes, both born in Frome, are living here. Alfred was a wool stapler. William George Brown, a widower born in Frome in 1827, was an architect, master builder, and a member of the building firm (see under No. 4). He designed some of the buildings which his brother built, including the rebuilding of St John's Church, extensions to Christ Church, and the old Market Hall (now the Cheese & Grain building). He is listed as living here in the 1871 census, together with his children: Mary Jane 16, Henry George 14 (both born in Isleworth), Emily Dora 10, Herbert George 8, and Annie Lydia 7, together with his unmarried niece Sophia Gough 28, and a servant, and again in the 1879 directory. By 1882 he is at 2 Fromefield, later at 7 Weymouth Road, and then at St Martin's, Park Road, which he probably designed, and where he died in July 1911. An obituary in the *"Somerset Standard"* lists his work and he was buried in St John's churchyard.

William Woodman from Hemel Hempstead, an unmarried brewer aged 24, is listed here in the 1881 census, with one servant and a boarder. Frederick Kirbell is listed as tenant in the 1886 auction of the Wickham estate, when the property was described as: *"That well built dwellinghouse No. 8 Willow Vale* (now No. 15), *with the garden in the rear, and a plot in front, pleasantly situate and joining the last lot* (No. 7 now No. 14), *now in the occupation of Mr Kirbell. This house contains capital cellars and scullery, 2 sitting rooms, large kitchen, china pantry, 2 bedrooms, dressing room, and 3 attics. The doors at the rear of this lot and lot 6 into lot 8 will be walled up by the vendors before the completion of the purchases."* It was sold after the auction to Mr Walter Harrold for £200.

Police superintendent Edward Deggan, born in Clifton, moved to 15 Willow Vale on his retirement, and is listed in the 1889 Poor Rate and 1891 census with his wife Matilda 58, and daughter Matilda Mary Deggan 21, a music teacher, together with his sister-in-law Mary Ayres 60, all born in Frome. By 1894 they had moved to 16 Somerset Road.

William Thick junior, born c1842 is named as resident in the 1894 directory and continues to occupy the house until 1907. His son George William Thick is shown in the 1910 voters list and directories for 1910 and 1912. In 1909 he succeeded to his father's watchmaker and silversmith business at 8 The Bridge, which continued to trade until at least 1931, but by 1921 he was living at 27 Somerset Road.

William Hedley Stokes was the next occupier, having lived at 7 Victoria Road in 1903 and then 5 Wallbridge Villas 1905-1919 before moving here in 1920. He purchased the freehold for £600 on 20th February 1924, which he sold on 31st May 1927, when he moved to Crossway, Rodden Road. Born at Trowbridge he came to Frome as a young man on his appointment as clerk of the Wallbridge Cloth Mills of Messrs A H Tucker Ltd. Subsequently he was appointed Secretary of the company, a position he held until his death in 1933. He was permanently identified with the musical life of Frome, and was a brilliant musician, excelling as a conductor, and in the arrangement of parts. He was first associated with C J Sage in an orchestral band that played for several years in the town and district. He then took over conductorship of the old Volunteers' Band, which ultimately formed the nucleus of the Frome Town Military Band, of which he was honorary conductor, and of which he was justifiably proud. One of the leading members of the Frome Operatic and Dramatic Society, he acted as honorary deputy conductor under Colonel F A Shaw, and succeeded the latter after his death. He took his dog out for a run from his Berkley Road home at 10 am on Christmas night and on his return was taken with a seizure from which he died a few hours afterwards on 26th December 1933.

Bernard Joseph Mitchell was born in Frome c1864, and in 1881 was living with his uncle, James Frappell at Clifton, where he was employed as a clerk. He had lived at 17 Willow Vale between 1891 and 1894 and 3 Willow Vale between 1903 and 1927. In 1927 he purchased No. 15 Willow Vale for £850 and enjoyed living here. Sadly his tenure was brief, for he died on 30th May 1928. His obituary reads:

"He had been failing in health for several months and had temporarily given up work in the hope that the rest might assist his recovery. Local life for Frome will be decidedly poorer by his death, so closely and certainly was he identified with it. He was a man of marvellous energy and thoroughness. Those two qualities he brought to bear not only in his business but in his hobbies and recreations, for he liked to regard the arduous and detailed work which he did for sporting and other institutions. He was a special Frome man and loved the old town and everything pertaining to its history and development. For a major part of his life he was the trusted, confidential servant of the late A R Baily, and was associated with him in the formation of the flourishing firm of E Baily & Son Ltd of which he was secretary and one of its directors. He was a man of great taste and culture, which he manifested in the acquirement of old furniture and china. He was a pioneer of photography, and helped to form and carry on the old Frome Camera Club. His own work bore the stamp of an artist. He travelled extensively and took many views of wonderful charm and beauty, some of which gained for him notable prizes and honours. It is difficult to enumerate all the sporting and other institutions with which Mr Mitchell was at one time or another in his life actively connected, but we can recall the Cricket Club, the Rugby Club, the Mechanics Institution and the Operatic Society. With Mr J Ace Banyon he founded the Bowling Club, and for years was its esteemed secretary and treasurer. A few years have passed since the members gave him practical proof of their deep appreciation of his services."

After a requiem Mass at St Catharine's, celebrated by his brother-in-law, Fr. Phillip Jackson, Bernard Mitchell was buried at Downside. His widow Enid (nee Jackson) had 3 brothers: Fr Phillip, Ernest and Wilfrid, and a sister, Mrs Moore. Enid died in 1959. She was survived by Fr. Jackson and Mrs Moore. Fr. Jackson died in 1966 aged 91, a year after celebrating the golden jubilee of his ordination as a priest. He had been a chaplain to the Forces during the First World War, and he spent some time at Chelsea before joining his sister at 15 Willow Vale. He often assisted Fr. Flyn, priest of St Catharine's Roman Catholic Church. He collapsed at home and died in the Victoria Hospital. After a requiem Mass at St Catharine's he was buried at Courfield near Ross-on-Wye. He was survived by his sister, and when she went to live in Rowden House, 15 Willow Vale was sold.

In today's parlance Colin Mayhew would be called a property developer, purchasing houses in need of renovation which he carried out whilst living in them. Whilst living at Tetbury he acquired 15 Willow Vale in September 1968 for £2,800, and moved here with his wife and 3 children. After the renovations were complete they moved to Great Hinton in Wiltshire.

The house was bought by Derek and Jean Gill, on 3rd January 1975 for £18,750, who moved here from 37 Beechwood Avenue. Their 3 sons enjoyed canoeing on the river and were amongst the first members of Frome Canoe Club. Derek was a teacher at Selwood School and Jean a State Registered Nurse. She had first visited the house in 1959 when Mrs Mitchell had been her patient.

16 WILLOW VALE

Originally part of No. 15, No. 16 appears to have been made into a separate dwelling early in the 19th century. Joseph Gainer was rated 8¼d in 1821 for a house, stable and workshop but had gone by 1827. Auctioneer Thomas Gough aged 40 was living here in 1841 with his wife Elizabeth 38, daughter Fanny 15, and sons William and Thomas George, both 11. Abraham Laverton is listed here in the 1846/1850 directories for a house and yard. It appears to have been uninhabited at the time of the 1851 census.

Richard Chappel is listed here in the 1858 rates. In the 1861 census Joseph Peacock 41, a railway contractor, his wife Elizabeth 41, their son James 18, an apprenticed engineer fitter (all born at Bitton in Gloucestershire), son Joseph 15, a saddler (born in Swansea), and daughters Elizabeth Ann 7, Ann 6 and Mary Jane 3 (all born in Frome) are listed as living here.

William Henry Penny 37, an ironmonger, is listed in the 1871 census, together with his wife Charlotte Ann 34 born at Queen Camel, and their 2 children, Francis Harry 6, born in Hampstead, Edith Kate 1, born in Frome, a servant and an apprentice. Joseph Ralph is mentioned in the 1879/1882 directories, and from the 1881 census we learn that he was 55 and a railway inspector. He and his wife Matilda 54 were both born in Wootton Bassett. Their children were Frederick 22, an engine fitter born in Reading, Augusta 17 born at Caversham, Albert 15 and Arthur 11, both born in Reading.

Agnes Doherty, a widow living on her own means was listed in the 1891 and 1893 directories, but by 1894 had moved to 7 The Bridge, and by 1907 to "Lomond" on Locks Hill. The 1891 census lists her with her children Winnie 11, born at Ayr in Scotland, sons Joseph 7, and James 4. Thomas Edwin Marshall was the occupier in June 1901 according to the deeds of No. 17. Elias Trowbridge Green was born in 1872 and is listed here in 1907. He married Adelaide Mary (1875-1961) and died in 1948. Both are buried at Holy Trinity. Edward Starr appears here in the 1910 voters list.

Thomas Budgett Gill is listed as occupier in 1917, having come from 25 Nunney Road, where he is found in 1912. He was born in Nunney and bought the freehold of the house from A M G Daniel on 20th April 1923, together with part of the strip of land stretching down to the river. He is still here in 1933, but by January 1935 had moved to "St Vincent", Cheddar.
T. B. Gill was organising secretary of the local branch of the Conservative Association. He died at Crockerton on 30th May 1938 having been agent for Lord Bath, and probably moved there at the time of his appointment.

In January 1935 the house was advertised for sale, and on 2nd February that year with "immediate possession". W Herrington is listed here in 1937.

Reginald Edgar Walwin was a tailor at 5/6 Palmer Street, son of the founder of the business, and moved here following its purchase by Frederick Walwin in 1935. He died on 5th November 1959, and his widow moved to 11 Bath Street, leaving the house unoccupied until its sale in 1993, shortly before her death. Peter Barnes purchased the property and moved here in August 1993. The house was almost unfit for habitation but he gradually restored it, firstly having the roof made sound and the windows restored. A musician, Peter used one of the rooms as a workshop in which he made harpsichords and other stringed instruments. With his partner, Jennifer Douglas, a textile artist, they had two sons, Robin and Gabriel. Christopher Bucklow and his wife Susan (nee Percival), bought the house on 23 June 1998 from Peter who had moved with his family to Rode and made substantial changes to the interior.

Residents gather to celebrate the approach of a new Millennium on 19th Dec 1999. Those pictured are: Jane MacGillivray with daughters Camilla and Mary, Beatrice MacGillivray, John & Jenny Buckley, Veronica & Basil Wilde, Jen & Kaz, John Cheetham, Chris & Sue Bucklow, Ray & Angela Daniel, Jean & Derek Gill, Alan & Gwenn Venn, Janice Leedam, Peter & Veronica Birch with daughters Ellie, Anna and Kitty.

Having worked as a curator at the Victoria & Albert Museum, Christopher became an artist and has exhibited widely in the UK, Australia, Canada and the USA. Sue was Curator of Photographs at the Hulton Archive, the archive of the Picture Post magazine, formerly the BBC Hulton Picture Library; this is now part of Getty Images. As a Photo Historian with an interest in local history Sue was chosen to research the J. W. Singer & Sons glass negatives at Frome Museum in 2001 and in 2009 initiated a display of photographs of the building of the Forth Bridge, celebrating its designer, the Frome born engineer Benjamin Baker

.

Their children, Beatrix (Bee) and Edward, were both born whilst they were living here. During renovations they discovered the name "Harriet Palmer" written several times on a bedroom wall with the date 1808. Mrs Prosser is listed in the 1810 rates when Nos. 15 and 16 was one house, and her relative or maid appears to have been practising her handwriting.

17 WILLOW VALE

The last property in Willow Vale began life as a workshop attached to the north-eastern end of the Queen Anne terrace. Purchased by the Great Western Railway Company, part of it was demolished to make way for the railway line. In 1858 the remaining portion was purchased by Joseph Peacock who converted it into a cottage. Lines in the stonework at first floor level in front and a blocked doorway and window facing the line indicate its former layout.

Mrs Henly is listed as a former occupier in the 1871 conveyance, and William Henry Penny, an ironmonger originally from Castle Cary as the actual occupier. Philip Wilshire 47, an accountant born at Challyhead Broughton in Wiltshire is listed in the 1879 and 1882 directories, and by the time of the

1881 census is living here with his wife Sarah 44, born in Frome, and their children George 12 and Amy 9, both born at Westbury.

W A Shady is listed as occupier in the 1886 sale. In the 1889 poor rate Frank Ashford's name has been substituted for Charles Maltby's, which has been crossed out. A coachman/groom from Witham Friary, he is listed in the 1891 census aged 47, with his wife Caroline 38 from Wanstrow, sons Henry Abner 14, a groom, John Yeoman 12, and Frank 10, and daughter Ada 8, all born at Witham Friary. B J Mitchell, a 27 year old commercial clerk was also living here in 1891 and is also listed at this address in the 1894 directory. By 1901 Henry Hodge is in occupation as G A Daniel's tenant, and bought the freehold from the latter's son on 20th April 1923 for £175. A gardener, Hodge died on 27th April 1944 at the age of 80. His daughter was Mrs Ethel Rawlings (1894-1973).

Alan Leslie Venn purchased the premises on 31st August 1951 for £1,000, having rented it for the previous year. Alan came here with his wife Gwynneth (Gwenn) and their son Simon. Their second son Paul was born here later that year. Alan built an extension on the side to create a hallway. The kitchen window is within a few feet from the railway line, and in the days of steam train drivers would sometimes stop and ask Gwenn to fill their kettle.

Alan was head of art at Oakfield School until failing eyesight caused him to take early retirement. He created a scene from Disney's *"Snow White and the Seven Dwarfs"* which was placed on the river bank by the Blue House and floodlit at Christmas time, much to the delight of the townspeople. Totally blind in his later years he died on 2nd December 2007 aged 94. Gwenn ran a playgroup at the house for many years. She lost her hearing and became profoundly deaf, but this did not restrict her sociability in any way. At the time of writing Gwenn is in her early 90s, spritely and still going strong.

THE TOWN MEADOW

Beyond the railway bridge the landscape opens out to become a broad vista of countryside with river, trees and meadow, skirted by the footpath to

Wallbridge. Its peace and tranquillity contrast with the hustle and bustle of the Town Centre. It is a joy to experience its seasonal changes. It has been threatened by a steady stream of planning applications for housing and other development but to date, these have all been resisted and long may it continue. Apart from being part of the river's flood plain, it is an environmental asset of great value to the town.

BIBLIOGRAPHY

Belham, Peter: *"The Making of Frome"* first published 1973 by F.S.L.S

Frome Library: *Census returns from 1841*
"Somerset Standard" and other local newspapers
held on microfilm

Frome Museum:*"1785 Survey of Households"*   (copy)

**Frome Society for
Local Study:** *Yearbooks and other publications*

Harding & Sons:*"Auctioneers Notebooks"* – Frome Museum

McGarvie, Michael, F.S.A: *"The Book of Frome",* published 1980 by Barracuda Books Ltd & *"Frome Place Names"*, first published by F.S.L.S in 1983

Griffiths, Carolyn: *"Dyeing the Blues"* & *"The Supply of Woad"*
During 2008/9 Carolyn researched the use of woad in Frome's dyeing industry, and organised a series of workshops and exhibitions. She quotes the following sources for the chapters she wrote for this book:

Hurry, J B: *"The Woad Plant and its Dye"* – Augustus M Kelly 1973

Olive, John: *"Shawford Mill Theatre"* and
"Notes on Shawford Mill", Private publication, 1977.

Parish, John: *"1810 letter"* – Royal Bath and West of England Society

Partridge, W: *"A Practical Treatise on Dyeing of Woollen, Cotton and Skein Silk"* 1823, Reprinted Pasold Research Fund Ltd, Edington, Wilts 1973

Householders: With thanks for access to *Deeds of specific properties*

St John's Church *Church Rates, Poor Rates & Parish Registers*

ILLUSTRATIONS

* By kind permission of Frome Museum

All other photographs are by John Buckley

THE 1785 SURVEY OF HOUSEHOLDS

Owner	Occupier	Males	Females
Households in Bridge Row:			
Henry Allen	John Langford, dyehouseman	1	2
John Adlam	John Adlam, baker	4	6
"	Will Palmer, painter	3	2
"	John Blatchley, labourer	1	0
"	James Clark, clockmaker	2	0
"	John Stevens, breeches maker	4	1
"	James Palmer, shearman	4	3
Households in Pilly Vale:			
Mary Gifford	Robert Bickle, gent	2	1
"	Elizabeth Ford, 2 maiden ladies (sic)	0	2
M. Griffiths	Jane Griffiths, widow	0	3
"	James Underhill, dyehouseman	1	2
"	Steven Guy, dyehouseman	2	2
"	Robert Carpenter, dyehouseman	1	1
"	John Wise, dyehouseman	2	2
"	Whittingtons, 3 maidens	0	3
"	Robert Francis, dyehouseman	4	4
"	Joseph Francis, dyehouseman	1	2
"	James Rogers, dyehouseman	3	3
"	William Cuzner, dyehouseman	2	1
"	John Blatchley, shearman	1	2
Mrs Beard	Bennett, labourer	3	3
"	Sam Corp, dyehouseman	1	3

A copy of this Survey is held in Frome Museum

RESIDENTS OF UNKNOWN ADDRESS

The people listed below appear in census and other records between the house numbers and in the years shown. They could have been living at either address, or in a property not yet identified.

Dates	House Nos.	Residents:
1821-7	11-WVH	Betty Fisher, laundress (possibly at WV house)
1827	Dyers-14	Charles Richards
1827	WVH-14	William Joyce
1841	2-3	John Palmer 70 weaver & wife Elizabeth 80
1841-6	5-6	John Thorne 40, labourer and wife Elizabeth, wool picker
1841	6-7	Hellery Gurney 75 female
1841	17-	Thomas Tetley 60 mason
1846	5-6	Ben Dyer
1851	2-3	John Summers 70 widower, pauper, and former shearman and daughter Eliza 24, burler*.
1851	2-3	John Morgan 42 boot maker, wife Ann 34, burler* and daughter Louisa 6, scholar.
1871	6-7	James Payton 59, woollen weaver and wife Maria 53, wool sorter

* A burler picked knots off newly woven cloth, and a shearman provided the final finish.

INDEX

Harvey: Edward, 40
Hayman: Alfred G, 17
Haynes: Alfred & Ann, 71
Hedges: John, 1; John & Sheila, 38
Hemmett: Michael & Mary, 58
Henly: Mrs, 78
Henry: Arthur, 38
Herridge: Sarah, 19; William, 19
Herrington: W, 77
Hewitt, 60
Hewlett: Neil, 24
Hill: Ralph G, 43
Hiscocks: William, 17
Hiscox: B, 24
Hobbs: Kenneth, 44
Hodge: Henry, 79
Holdeway: Charles, 66
Hopkins: Gary, 61
Horler: Steve, 32
Hotchkin: Ralph, 65
House numbering, 12, 36
Huggins: Jill, 24; Rev. John, 24
Hugnell: William, 19
Hurden: Charles, 39
Hurry: J B, 81
Hutchins, 18
Huxley: Barbara, 24, 32
Jackson: Arthur J, 16, 17; Fr Phillip, 74; Geoffrey, 1; Geoffrey & Christine, 45
James: Duncan, 31; Eric, 61
Jeffries: Miss C M, 38; Peter & Veronica, 52
Jenkins: Steve, 61
Joyce: William, 55, 84
Kelly: Damien, 32, 34, 36; Roger, 44
Kemp, 37, 54
Kidelan: Paul A, 70
Kingett: Elizabeth, 41
Kirbell: Frederick, 72
Knight: Louisa, 23; M S, 35

Lamb Brewery, 21
Langford: John, 83
Laverton: Abraham, 75; H C, 35; Walter, 40
Lee: Alvan Jack, 39, 40, 41; Gary & Vivienne, 43
Leedam: Pip & Janis, 18
Leonard: Adrian, 20
Lewis: Mr & Mrs, 18
Lincoln: Miss, 60
Livery stables, 30, 33
Lloyd: Joyce Elizabeth, 58
Longleat Estate, 62
Loveridge: Susan, 24
Lupton: Eva & Dan, 61
Lush: Hugh, 36
MacArthur: Mrs GAV, 44; Mrs H, 44
Macey: James, 39, 54
MacGillivray: Beatrice, 33; Jane, 33
MacLeay: Alastair, 1
MacQueen: Peter, 38
Maidment: Anna & Lucy, 66
Maitland: Angus C M, 70
Maltby: Charles, 79
Maltings: Station, 21, 23, 56; W V, 19, 20, 21, 22, 23, 24, 56
Marsden, 18
Marshall: Thomas Edwin, 76
Massey: Ruth, 18
Mayhew: Colin, 75
McGarvie: Michael, 81
McNicoll: Alexander & Karen, 43
Miles: Sarah, 71
Mill: Fulling, 11; Shawford, 46, 47, 49, 81; Sheppard's, 10; Town, 7, 10, 43, 54, 55; Wallbridge, 33, 49, 73, 82
Mill House Court, 30
Millard: Enoch, 43
Mills: George, 39, 43
Millstream, 7

Millstream Coach House, 33
Miners: Arthur G, 35
Mitchell: B J, 23, 74, 79; Mrs, 75
Monk: George Edwin, 16
Moody: S, 58
Moon: George, 44
Moore: Mrs, 65, 74
Morgan: Charles, 43; John, 84
Mortimer: Ann, 62, 71
Mountier: C, 24
Mullett: Paul & Sheila, 44
Nash, 60; Brian & Helen, 58
Neale: Mrs Alice, 39; Mrs E, 39
Noad: cloth maker, 47
Norman: Eric, 36; W, 35
Norwell: S P, 20
Nutley: E H, 20
Old Coach House, 46, 50
Olive, 54, 55; Edmund Jnr, 67; Elizabeth, 37, 55; family, 10; John, 81; John V, 11, 34, 55; Maj John, 11, 26, 34, 36, 53, 54
Organ: Mrs A E, 35
Ormerod: Maria E, 57; Rev Charles, 57
Osborne: Angela, 61; Col G, 57
Padfield: Elizabeth, 55
Paget: Anne, 18; Herbert T, 17
Palmer: Anthony, 29; Charles, 16; Edgar & Nancy, 38; Edward, 16, 17; Harriet, 78; James, 26, 83; John & Elizabeth, 19, 84; Nicholas, 16; William, 16, 83
Parfitt: Anne, 40
Parish: John, 49, 81; William & Edward, 46
Parker, 18
Parsons: Alfred, RA, 67; Dr Frederick, 67; Dr Joshua, 67
Partridge: W, 81
Payton: James, 84
Peacock: Joseph, 75, 78

Peckham: Miss E M, 20
Penelhurn: John, 38
Penny: William Henry, 76, 78
Phillips: Dr Justin, 24; John, 16
Pilly: Vale, 6
Pinkard: A W, 52
Pollock: Jean, 36
Potter: John, 21
Powney: Edward & Bessie, 57
Pratten: James Wm., 35
Prosser: Mrs, 71, 78
Pudden: Hedley Joseph, 58
Purchase: D, 69
Quail: Julian, 32
Railway: Bridge, 5, 7, 79; Great Western, 8; Line, 8, 14, 50, 62, 78, 79
Ralph: Joseph, 76
Rathmell, 21; David & Kathleen, 24; Timothy, 24
Rawlings: Mrs Ethel, 79
Ray: John, 38
Richards: Charles, 55, 84; Mrs, 24
Rigg: & Vallis, architects, 57; Percy, 52, 59, 82
Riparian owners, 6
River Frome, 6, 11, 51, 60, 79
Riverside Terrace, 52, 59, 82
Robinson, 18
Rogers: Herbert, 40; James, 83
Roman: Sue, 18
Rose: N G & R A, 61
Sangar: Elizabeth, 68
Saunders: John, 16; Andrew & Penelope, 32
Scowcroft: Janet, 38
Sealy: Jane, 35
Shady: W A, 79
Shearmen, 14, 29, 83
Sheppard: family, 10; George, 10; Mrs Sarah Ann, 20; TBW, 36

Sheppard & Watson, 36, 41, 54, 55
Shingles: Fanny, 55
Shipley: Mrs, 24
Short: Mrs, 44
Singer: J W & Sons, 14, 31, 78
Smallbone-Masters: Rosaleen Tessy, 68
Smith: Christopher, 61; Eleanor, 32; Henry, 62; James, 62, 64; John, 54, 63; Margaret, 54; Michael, 62; Mrs, 17; Robert, 52, 54, 61; S A, 24; Thomas, 61
Smith Estate Act, 54, 63
Somerset Smithy, 11, 31
Somerset Standard, 8, 9, 18, 20, 27, 81
Spalding: Wilfred Frank, 69
Sparks: Mrs, 23; Thomas, 23
St John's Church, 6, 23, 51, 55, 66, 71, 72
Stafford: Mrs I K, 44
Starr: Edward, 76
Stearn: Jonathan, 61
Stevens: Arthur, 33, 39; John, 23, 83
Stile: George, 19
Stokes: William Hedley, 73
Stubbs: Simon, 20
Summers: John, 84
Summerscale: Kate, 67
Sustrans, 6
Sutton: Charles W, 17
Swan Brewery, 56
Taylor: Alfred, 55
Teller: Jo & Sue, 58
Tetley: Thomas, 84
The Old Kiln, 38
Thick: George William, 72; William, jnr., 72
Thomas: H F G, 24
Thompson: Ann Elizabeth, 68; Samuel & Sons, 24

Thorne: John, 43; John & Elizabeth, 84; Sarah, 44; William, 29
Tipper family, 33
Town Bridge, 5, 7, 13, 14, 42
Town Meadow, 5, 10, 79
Treasure: Ivor H, 39
Tubbs: George, 28
Tucker: Edwin, 37; George, 37; Messrs A H, 73
Tuffs: P, 52
Tunnels, 45, 51, 52
Turner: Mr & Mrs E J, 29
Underhill: James, 83
Underwood: G. A., 13; Sophia, 34
Vaters: James, 23; Thomas, 23
Venn: Alan & Gwenn, 79
Vining: Rev F W, 23
Wall: family, 30; Fanny, 28; Thomas, 27
Walwin: Frederick, 36, 38, 44, 77; Jeremy, 1, 41, 43; Reginald Edgar, 77; Roy, 82
Warehouses, 5, 10, 25, 30, 36, 41, 54, 82
Warwick: Jessie, 38
Watts: James, 40; Miss L G, 20
Weaver: Mrs, 70
Wessex Retirement Homes, 38
Wheeler: Miss F, 20; Walter, 20
White: Brothers, 41; John, 11, 31
Whitehead: Andrew, 68
Whitmarsh: Frederick, 39, 43
Whittington: Misses, 83
Wickham: Estate, 72; James Anthony, 63, 71; James WDT, 63
Wild: Basil, 1, 51; Basil & Veronica, 50; Harry, 50
Wildlife, 10
Wilkins: Sarah, 37
Wilkinson: Derek, 70
Willis: Mark, 24
Willmott:, Geoffrey, 32